THE HIRO MATSUDA STORIES
Samurai Spirit

STEPHANIE KOJIMA

Copyright © 2019 Stephanie Kojima
All rights reserved.

ISBN-13: 978-1-7309-1895-7

DEDICATION

For Hiro Matsuda
legendary wrestler
inspirational man
loving husband and father

CONTENTS

Acknowledgments

1	Introduction	1
2	Growing Up	3
3	The First Days of Wresting	10
4	On My Own	17
5	Flying Free	22
6	Mexico	29
7	Living the Dream	45
8	Vacation in Mexico	54
9	Kansas City	56
10	Oklahoma	59

CONTENTS

11	Florida	77
12	Training with Karl Gotch	91
13	Back In Florida	94
14	The Return Home	98
15	Back In America	101
16	Tennessee	104
17	1965 - 1967	106
18	North Carolina	112
19	Florida 1969 - 1987	119
20	Atlanta	135
21	World Superstar Wrestling	140

ACKNOWLEDGMENTS

Thank you to my mother, Judy Kojima, and my sister, Heather Kojima Proud, for their loving support. Thank you to John, my amazing husband, for his technical support and words of encouragement. Thank you to Osamu Nishimura for helping me correctly spell the Japanese words. Thank you to Jorge Martinez for helping with the Spanish names. Thank you to Rev. Billy C. Wirtz. Our chance meeting and conversation about my dad ignited the desire to publish the stories.

1 INTRODUCTION

Sweat slings off his golden brown skin as he repeatedly jump squats down and back counting in Japanese to 500, the first set. Wearing the black trunks, white socks, and tennis shoes, Hiro Matsuda sternly watches his reflection in the sliding glass door on his back porch. Then, it is Hindu push-ups, regular push-ups, sit ups, leg lifts, bridges, and more jumping squats. Today is July 22. Hiro Matsuda's 61st birthday. He pushes himself to do the exact same work-out he did in his twenties. He is determined to prove his stamina. Hiro Matsuda will accept nothing less from himself.

Judy glances at him once in a while concerned. She is in the kitchen cooking tapioca pudding. Hiro doesn't eat sweets except a bowl of tapioca pudding on his birthday and the occasional scoop of pralines and cream ice cream. Judy has stood by Hiro's side for 36 years through all the ups and downs of the wrestling business. She is his Lady in the Blue Dress he saw from the ring while he was strutting around showing off his sexy muscular legs. She thinks about their daughters wishing they could all be together. Heather is in Venice Beach, California. Stephanie is in San Diego. Each will call later to wish her daddy "happy birthday".

In February 1999, Hiro came down with the flu. He was never one to go to the doctor, but when he wasn't recovering as usual, he succumbed to the urgings of his wife and his sister to go to the doctor. He received the routine tests for a man his age. During the colonoscopy, the procedure had to be stopped due to a blockage, and Hiro was immediately admitted to the hospital for surgery. Tumors were found in his colon, abdomen, and liver. The surgeon removed all possible, but his liver was three-quarter consumed already. The doctor told Judy the bad news, colon cancer that had metastasized throughout the abdominal cavity. He suggested to wait to tell Hiro until he recovered from the surgery. Devastated, Judy summoned the courage to call their daughters, one of the worst phone calls to ever make. Heather and Stephanie immediately flew to Tampa.

Hiro had his women around him while he recovered. The doctor still did not want to tell Hiro that he had cancer and the prognosis was not good. The doctor's view was that if he tells him now, Hiro could become depressed and not recover from surgery as quickly. He did not know the spirit of Hiro Matsuda. Hiro was a fighter; knowledge was power for him. Also, Judy and his daughters could not sit with Hiro by his hospital bed holding that knowledge secret. It felt wrong. Their family bond was close and honest.

After much arguing with the doctor, he was finally persuaded. He reluctantly told Hiro the results of the surgery and that he had cancer. Hiro received the news with a stoic face, still body, slight hand trembling the only sign of the weight of the news. He asked the doctor, " How long do I have to live?" The doctor replied, "No one can tell you that." The family sat in silence after the doctor left. Then, Hiro said," Get me a book about positive thinking and a book about death."

While Hiro Matsuda was receiving treatment for the cancer, he decided to tell his family his life stories. In the evening after dinner, the family sat down together and Hiro reflected upon his life. Judy learned about Hiro's early wrestling days when they dated. After marriage, she was along for the ride of the business. Heather and Stephanie, as Hiro Matsuda's daughters, were sheltered from the wrestling business for their protection. As a heel Hiro made many fans hate him. His motto was the more the fans hated him, the better the show, and the better the draw. Also, he followed the Japanese custom of keeping family and business separate. Therefore, these evening talks were the first time Heather and Stephanie heard who Hiro Matsuda truly was. To them he had been "Daddy", the loving, supportive father who always expected the best from them.

The following are the stories Hiro Matsuda told in his own words. The events, dates, and names are as he recalled them. If there are mistakes, it is unintentional. Imagine sitting across from Hiro Matsuda. He begins to tell his life story. He begins with his birth.

2 GROWING UP

    This is Hiro Matsuda telling my life story. I was born on July 22, 1937 in Yokohama. Since my mother was a small woman, only about five feet tall, she could not give birth by the natural way. She had to have a cesarean. I weighed a little more than ten pounds. When I was born, the head doctor of the hospital came to visit my mother. He told her, "Your baby is the biggest baby in this hospital!" Then, he patted my head and gave her a big smile. This is what my mother told me.
    In 1937 my parents owned a little vegetable store. They were living in the depression era, during the time of the war against China. All Japanese had a hard time making a living. My father went to the wholesale vegetable market every day. My mother carried me on her back while taking care of the vegetable store. My father would load vegetables on a rickshaw; then, travel door to door in the neighborhood selling vegetables.
    When I was close to one year old near the end of 1937, my father was called to the army service. He had to go to China. He left home for a while in order to train to go to China. One day my mother was told by my father's regiment that he would come close to town on the train. From the window of the train, my father saw my mother and called to her. He wrapped a Japanese flag around a stone. He threw it to her, so at least she could have something to keep in memory of him. They did not know if they would see each other again. This is the story I was told. We were very fortunate. After seven months of duty in China, my father was sent home, because he had a wife and son waiting for him. Many of his friends never returned home. When he came home, we had a wonderful

time working together. We were poor, living day by day, but happy to be with each other.

*****

My father told me a story of my first adventure. In our neighborhood every Sunday there was a brass band that played to lead people to promote Christianity. My parents were busy in the store, and did not notice their son leave on an adventure. When my father realized I was missing, they looked all over the neighborhood. Finally, my father came to the church looking for me. He entered the church and saw the little geta, wooden shoes that I wore. He found me among the little boys in the crowd listening to the music.

*****

When I was about three years old, my father took me to the Yokohama-shi Kanagawa Village where he was born. There was a man who was a doctor, a palm reader, and an herbalist. My father wanted to know about me and my future. The doctor looked at my palm. He said, "This boy is not going to shit in your house." This saying meant that I would leave his home. My father was so angry. He asked, " How do you know when my boy grows up that he will leave my house? He is only three years old!" My father did not like what he had heard, but the doctor had been correct.

*****

In first grade I was a very big boy. Sumo wrestling is a popular Japanese sport. Even in grammar school, once a year there was a sumo tournament. I participated in the tournament. I beat fifteen boys in a row. This is the story my father told me. I do not remember this.

*****

In 1941 Japan attacked the United States at Pearl Harbor. People in Japan worked very hard in support of the Japanese army and navy to try to win the war. We did not know anything about the war; the propaganda told us we were winning. However, the truth was our country was getting worse. At the end of 1943, the first B29 attack came to Japan. My family lived in an industrial area, and my parents feared that an air bombing would kill me. They sent me to the countryside where my father was born. I was a little boy who did not understand why my parents would send me away to my uncle's house. I wanted to stay with my mother and father.

My father was born in Yokohama-shi Kanagawa. When I lived there, only a few farm houses existed and the rest of the land was rice patties. Today, the rice patties have become housing projects. I went to visit a few years ago to try to find the memories of my childhood, but I could not recognize the place. Everything was different.

In my young mind, I thought I was sent away because I did something wrong. I felt very guilty. During the day I went to grammar school in the countryside. I made friends with other children. Playing with friends occupied my mind in the day, but at night I remembered my mother and father. I was told I cried every night. I felt independent during the daytime. I had many boys following me; I was a leader. Unfortunately at night, I was a little boy crying all the time.

During the stay at my uncle's house, even in the countryside, we had United States B29 bombardments every night. We would hide in the bomb shelter the army made deep in the mountain like a big tunnel. I remember for a few hours the bombs would drop, shaking the ground around the tunnel. The next morning all the kids ran to see where the bombs dropped. The craters were enormous, and in a few days they would fill with water. We used to swim in the B29 bomb craters. All the kids enjoyed it. It was great fun.

In grammar school, every morning the children gathered for assembly in the playground. Every morning the principal gave us this sermon. "The Japanese Imperial Army is winning against the United States. All children growing up, you must be very patriotic. You have to sacrifice for the Japanese country, for our Motherland." I believed it. All children believed it.

*****

I have a vivid memory that I am ashamed to tell. I went with two friends to the train station. We were three little boys who wanted sweet candy so badly, but we did not have any money. In those days there were not many stores, because of the American bombings. Temporary stores stood around the train station. I saw one store that had caramels made from melted sugar. I made a decision that I would steal them. The other boys working with me distracted the owner, and I stole the caramels. I shared them with the other two boys. For some reason, one of the boys snitched to the schoolteacher. I was so afraid that I would get disciplined. Fortunately, before I was reprimanded by the schoolteacher, my parents moved me back to their house. They never knew of the trouble.

*****

The war ended. My parents decided to move to a different place. They found a small vegetable field, built a small shack, and started a vegetable stand. I was very happy to be back with my mother and my father. We had hard times. If we could have something to eat, we were lucky. Most of the time we had only a small amount of rice. My mother would make rice with mostly water, sometimes a few vegetables. We filled our stomachs with more liquid than substance. We did not complain; everyone was in the same situation.

I started a new school by my home. My father took me the first day to introduce me to the teacher and students. I was happy to escape being disciplined by my old schoolteacher. Plus, meeting new kids was very exciting. One day at school, I fought with another boy. I came home crying. I remember my father saying to me, "A boy never cries when coming home; this means you have no honor." After that moment, I never lost a fight with anyone. I was a big boy among the other children, and I became the leader in this school, too. I remember all the kids obeying my orders.

My father woke up before sunrise to go to the countryside to look for vegetables. When I became ten years old, my father started to take me with him. I was a strong, tall boy at ten. He rode his bicycle with me sitting on the handlebars. In the countryside we gathered vegetables to take home. Then, we would take them to Tokyo to sell them for a good price. I carried a large backpack filled with vegetables, and my father carried a larger backpack. We walked one and a half miles to Tsurumi Station, took the train for thirty minutes to Shinbashi, and then walked to the vegetable market. My father used to make a great profit. After he sold the vegetables, we would stop by the noodle stand. He used to buy me noodles. I remember being a little boy always hoping my father would buy me noodles after we worked hard selling vegetable.

*****

I fell in love for the first time in fifth grade. Our neighbor came to buy vegetables at my parents' every evening. The daughter of our neighbor was my classmate, and she was the most beautiful girl. Her name was Masako. I thought I wanted to marry her. She did not know I loved her. One day in school, another boy teased her until she cried. I was so angry I rushed at the boy. I beat the hell out of him! I rescued my love. While buying vegetables one night at my parents' stand, her mother told my parents they were going to move to a location about fifteen miles away. Her daughter would have to go to a different school. When I heard this news, my heart was broken. At school Masako asked me, "Kojimasan, will you draw a picture for me to keep for a memory?" I was a good drawer when I was a young boy. I drew pictures for her and she was happy. Then, the time came to say good-bye. Her family moved to their new home.

*****

I played baseball when I was in junior high school. I attended Sueyoshi Junior High School. In those days, baseball and sumo wrestling were the only sports in Japan. I dreamed of becoming a professional baseball player. I practiced with intense discipline. Yokohama had more than 100 junior high schools. Every spring and autumn, we had a school tournament. My school team won the Tsurumi region; then, we had to travel to a different region to compete with another school. We played against Kanagawa Junior High School. The tournament happened to be near my first love Masako's new home. We played a good baseball game, and we won. After the game, I took a different way back so I could search for Masako's house. I found her house, but stood there a few moments just looking. I did not have the guts to go knock on the door.

I spent my time in junior high school playing baseball and studying very hard. I was accepted to a prestigious mechanical engineer high school, Shokojishu. I was also invited to Ebara High School in Tokyo to play baseball. I passed the examination to attend Ebara, but I chose to go to Shokojishu. I continued to study intensely and play baseball. It was difficult to concentrate on both. I would wake up early, train hard for baseball, go to school, attend practice for baseball, return home for dinner, and spend time studying. All my heart was set on playing baseball. After three months attending Shokojishu, I asked my father if I could change high schools. I wanted to go to Ebara High School in Tokyo. My father told me that it was my choice, my future life. He wrote a resignation letter for me. The school gave me permission to move to Ebara High School.

The dream of the Ebara High School baseball team was to compete in Osaka Koshien Baseball Stadium where all the high schools played to find out who is number one. First, we had to become the champions of Tokyo which meant we had to beat 400 high schools in Tokyo. When I was a sophomore, we went to the finals, but unfortunately we lost the final game. At that time I was not playing; I was only a supporter. In my junior year, I became a regular team member. My position was pitcher and left field. I played with all my heart. We went to the semi-finals, but we lost. Our school always came close, but we never won the championship of Tokyo.

*****

While playing baseball in high school, I was hoping to play professionally or to be scouted by a college. It was during my senior year that I saw professional wrestling on television for the first time. In those days, not everyone had a TV. The television was in the train station or the noodle house or some business. I remember vividly there was a huge person like I had never seen wrestling against Rikidozan, one of the top Japanese professional wrestlers at that time. The huge person was one of the Sharpe Brothers, Ben or Mike Sharpe. They both were six feet, six inches tall, about 300 pounds. When I saw the dynamic of profession wrestling, I said to myself,

"That is it! I want to become a professional wrestler." I was eighteen years old, a senior in high school.

*****

During the summer our school uniforms were extremely hot. The school had a tradition of uniforms that was over 100 years old. The students wanted to change this tradition, but the administration and the teachers were against change. The students decided to hold a gathering to change the school uniforms. My baseball coach was also the vice principal. He told his team, "You are members of the baseball team and you are not going to participate in the student gathering!" When someone told me "Do not", it was my nature to rebel. I volunteered to participate in the student gathering. I did not care about playing baseball anymore, because professional wrestling was in my heart now. I resigned from the team. Our student gathering was successful. The summer school uniforms were changed to be cooler and more comfortable. Also, I had seized the opportunity to change my future from professional baseball to professional wrestling.

*****

When I was growing up after the war in 1945 to 1952, there were many American soldiers staying in Japan for the Occupation. They seemed to be very rich. They had abundant food. They had candy, chocolate, and chewing gum that they gave to the children sometimes. They had more money than we did. Even on the train, they had their own special car. I wondered what kind of country could America be to have so much abundance. I told myself, "One day I will go to the United States." That was why I was so entranced when I saw professional wrestling. I thought this could be the way to see the world and to get to America. I thought if I stay in Japan to go to college, then I will be stuck on a little island living within the structured system. I would go nowhere. Now, the dream alive in my heart was to become a professional wrestler and see the world.

3 THE FIRST DAYS OF WRESTLING

On April 1, 1956 I graduated from Ebara High School. Most of my friends went to college to play baseball or to study for their future. However, I wanted to become a professional wrestler. I decided to visit Rikidozan.

He was the first professional wrestler of Japan. During the American Occupation, entertainment was sent from America for the soldiers staying in Japan. Part of the entertainment they brought was a group of wrestlers. At that time there was Bobby Brown and Harold Sakata from Hawaii. Sakata was the 1948 weight lifting Olympic champion. When they came to Japan, they discovered Rikidozan; he had retired from sumo wrestling. Rikidozan went to Hawaii to train to become the first professional wrestler from Japan. That was his story.

I was a young boy with a big dream going to visit Rikidozan's house. I did not go alone; I was too scared. Two high school friends accompanied me for moral support, but I was the only one who wanted to become a professional wrestler. I knocked on the door. My heart was pounding. A young wrestler opened the door and asked us what we wanted. "I want to become a professional wrestler," I said. He looked at me from head to toe. "You have good size. Come in," he told me. At eighteen I stood six feet and one inch tall. I weighed 187 pounds.

Lunch was being served when I arrived. When the young wrestler led me into the dining room I could not believe what I saw. The table was overflowing with food. There was beef and chicken. I had never eaten meat. My family could not afford to buy meat. Rikidozan was sitting at the table. He looked at me and said, "Young boy, you have to eat." I forced myself to eat as much as I could.

That was the first time I tasted beef. I was so happy to be eating so much food. After lunch Rikidozan said, "You want to become a professional wrestler. Tomorrow, you come to my gym." It was June 1956. I started professional wrestling.

After Rikidozan accepted me, I went home to tell my father that I was going to become a professional wrestler. He was surprised. My father said very seriously, "Whatever you choose to do, never fail. Do not look back from what you choose."

I trained every day. In the morning I helped my father go to the vegetable market. After lunch I went to Rikidozan's gymnasium. I trained very hard pushing weights. Two wrestlers, Yoshihara and Yoshino Sato, were my trainers. They became my good friends, too. They were about seven years older than I. Yoshihara had graduated from a prestigious college. He was a member of their amateur wrestling team, and he was the second in the welter weight at college. Yoshino Sato had been a sumo wrestler. He quit at the same time as Rikidozan. They belonged to the same club of sumo. Yoshihara and Yoshino Sato trained me every day. They took me in like a little brother, but they beat me every day! We would spend two to three hours in the ring. I tried with all my strength and strategy to beat them, but for six months I always ended up on my shoulders and my back pinned down to the mat. I tried the best I could.

The summer of 1956 I participated in my first wrestling tour. I was nineteen years old, and it was a time I could never forget. American wrestlers named Tom Rice, Lucky Sonavitch, and another wrestler whose name I cannot remember wrestled against Rikidozan, Toyonoboli, Yoshino Sato, and Azumafuji. I was not wrestling yet. My job was to be a second to the American wrestlers. This meant I guided them to the ring before the match, and back to the dressing room after the match. I could speak some English, because I learned it in high school. My responsibilities also included helping to build the wrestling ring and to break it down. Then, we put the ring in the truck for the next town.

This was my first time travelling all over Japan. From Northern Japan to Southern Japan, we travelled from tip to tip of the country. I had a wonderful time riding on the train. Growing up in Tokyo and Yokohama, I did not see much of the countryside. Being part of the tour gave me the opportunity to see how the people in the country lived. Even though I was only a second and I helped build the ring, I was part of the team. When we went to the small towns, I was like a little star. In those days, rice farmers or fishermen lived in the countryside. We rode on an old-fashioned steam engine train. At every station we had to stop. All the young boys did not have seats. We sat and slept on newspapers on the floor. I did not mind, because I always had a stomach full of food and I was seeing the different towns.

*****

That summer tour gave me great memories, especially from the time in Shikoku Island. We took a boat trip that was about three hours from Osaka. The city was called Tokushima. All the wrestlers stayed in a nice hotel, but the ring team stayed in a small hotel ran by a family. A mother and father owned and operated the hotel with the help of their two daughters. We had one day off when we arrived to the town. The family invited all the boys to the beach. We had a great time relaxing and visiting with each other and our new friends. The next day we had the show. The ring team went early to the arena to build the ring. I did the same job as second for the American wrestlers. When the match was over, we broke down the ring and returned to our hotel for the night. The family had prepared a delicious meal for us. After dinner, we were invited to a nightclub. The two daughters went with us.

The younger daughter named Chizuko Miki was a beautiful girl. She was a year younger than I. I did not know how to dance, but the first time I danced with her she taught me how. My heart was pounding; I was so nervous. We had a great time dancing. Somehow, I just fell in love with her in one night.

The morning came and it was time to go to the next city. The family came with us to the train station to say good-bye to their customers. My heart was with my new love. I was looking out the window at her as the train was pulling away from the station. She was getting smaller and smaller, and my heart was getting sadder and sadder. When I returned to Tokyo, my heart was still with Chizuko Miki.

On the tour, I earned my own money for the first time. I went to the jewelry store to order a necklace with her initials on it. I wrapped it in tissue paper, and sent the gift to my love. A few days later I received a package from her. When I opened it, there was a wallet with a letter. I never had the opportunity to see her again. However, I still have the little wallet she gave me, and I have a wonderful memory of my love.

*****

After the summer tour ended, my training with Yoshihara and Yoshino Sato began again. I trained every day dreaming of becoming the best wrestler in Japan and of going to the United States. My day started in the vegetable store where I helped my father and mother until noon. Then, I took the bus from Tsurumi Station to Tokyo Station. I wanted to save 30 yen to buy a bowl of noodles, so from Tokyo Station I walked about 25 minutes to Rikidozan's gym. Once I arrived at the gym, we trained hard for about five hours. My reward, as well as the part of the day I anticipated, was a restaurant dinner provided by Yoshihara and Yoshino Sato. They took all the young boys training to become wrestlers so they could eat a lot of food to grow strong and to increase weight. They bought me a couple of Kirin beers, and they would tell me, "Kojima, you must eat as much food as you can. You have to get big!" My weight was 187 pounds; then, 192 pounds; then, 220 pounds. I ate huge amounts of food! I do not know where all the food went in my stomach, because I was so skinny at first. Yet, I was a young boy with a fast metabolism, and I was training hard every day. All the food could not stick to my bones!

The hard training consisted of preparing to wrestle and then wrestling in the ring. We warmed up with calisthenics. Next, we did body building by pushing weights. Then, we focused on leg exercises, mainly squats. I used to do 1,000 squats without stopping. We spent one hour and a half preparing to wrestle; then, we went to the ring. Yoshihara and Yoshino Sato wrestled against me in the ring. They took turns and I worked the entire time alone. I dreamed to beat those two. I tried the best I could, but every time I would end up on my back. I got up and tried again. After six months of ending up on my back, I finally took the two guys down. That was the first enjoyment I ever experienced in my training. They told me, "Kojima, you did good." I was so happy when I heard those words.

I had the same routine every day. Once in a while on Saturday, we did a half day of training, and then we went to the baseball park.

Most everyone enjoyed playing baseball. I loved to play baseball with the other wrestlers. Many of them did not know how to play, so they liked me to be on their team. My position was pitcher, and my team usually won. This was my relaxing, fun time. The rest of my time I concentrated with all my heart and my mind on wrestling.

At the end of 1956, and at the beginning of the new year 1957, another wrestling tour came to Japan. This tour started in Okinawa. All the big famous top wrestlers flew from Tokyo to Okinawa, but the young boys like me took the train. I was not a wrestler yet; I still helped build the ring. The train ride took about twelve hours. It was an old time train, so it took a long time to reach our destination. But, I was a young boy enjoying every minute of the scenery, because it was different from the northern part of Japan. The train traveled from Tokyo, passed Osaka, then Kobe, and then stopped in Sannomiya. We took a 1500 ton ferry boat from Sannomiya to Okinawa which was a three day trip. The first day the sea was very calm, but when the boat left New Japan going between Kyushu and Okinawa the waves were getting bigger and bigger. My stomach was going up and down, up and down. Everything I ate, I threw up. I could not keep any of the food in my stomach. I stayed in bed until we reached Naha, Okinawa. At that time, Okinawa was an American Occupation. All the taxi cabs were brand new American cars, and they drove on the right side of the street. The rest of Japan drove on the left side. The money was different, too. It was a special kind of dollar used in the American Occupation.

Finally, we arrived in the Naha port. When I stepped from the boat to the land, I could not walk straight. I felt as if I was drunk. It took me thirty minutes to adjust to walking on the land. The first day all the wrestlers had off, but we young boys had to build the ring for the show. We were having a three day show at the Naha Baseball Stadium. After we finished our work, we went to the hotel where the ring builders stay. We were so hungry from our hard work. This was my first opportunity to try Okinawan food. We all stuffed ourselves with delicious food; then, we went back to our hotel to rest for the show on the next day.

The first day of the shows came. The Naha Baseball Stadium held about 12,000 people, and the place was sold out. There was the wrestling ring, but no chairs. The people sat on mats on the floor. This was the first professional wrestling show they would experience.

The first match was Rikidozan against Algerian Bear John, the Canadian champion. Then, the other matches followed. The first day was beautiful; everyone was happy. On the second day, we had a sold out show again. During one of the matches, two challengers came to the ring. One was a karate expert with five black belts. One was a marine from Hawaii. They challenged Rikidozan, the biggest wrestling star in Japan. Rikidozan told me, "Kojima, you go in the ring and take care of those two guys." I had nothing to lose. I had confidence I could beat both the guys, because this was my great opportunity to show my hard training by Yoshihara and Yoshino Sato. The first guy I had to fight was a karate fifth black belt. He was ready when I stepped into the ring. I looked at him straight and deep into his eyes. I told him, "Do your best. This is between me and you. We fight until win or lose or die." He knew I was ready to go. I moved like a cat. He tried to hit me. I yelled, "Hit me as hard as you can!" I blocked my face, but he kicked me in the stomach. My stomach was like a rock; the kick didn't bother me. I said to him, "Can you hit me harder?" I laughed. I went in for the attack. He tried to hit me again. I blocked his hand, then threw him to the mat. BAM! He hit the mat hard and I was on top of him. I grabbed his neck cracking like it was going to break. He was screaming, "Stop! Stop! Stop!" Then, I realized. All of a sudden, I realized all the people were watching me. The match was over. I had won. My opponent whimpered out of the ring. I looked over at the next challenger. I looked straight into his eyes and yelled, "You! You are next! Come in the ring and fight!" He said to me, "I will have nothing to do with you!" I felt so proud. The whole crowd was cheering for me. A nineteen year old boy, 192 pounds, all muscle.

The show was over. I went to the dressing room feeling very proud. I was hoping Rikidozan would praise me for the victory. As soon as he saw me in the dressing room, he slapped my face a couple of times. I had no idea why he slapped me. He shouted, "Kojima! Why didn't you play around with that karate guy longer?" I thought to myself, " I was fighting for my life for you!" I did not say this, because I must respect my sensei. I was boiling mad, infuriated. I wanted to rage an attack on him. Toyonoboli, another big wrestler in Japan, saw my anger. He grabbed me and carried me away. He told me, "Master Rikidozan was very happy with your performance, but he does not know how to show his appreciation to you. That is the way he is." To me this did not matter, I lost full respect for him.

The three day show was successful. After the third night match, the promoter invited us to the Okinawa geisha house. We ate a delicious dinner made of the most beautiful food, and after dinner we enjoyed entertainment by the Okinawan geishas. It felt so great to be a young, handsome boy surrounded by so many girls. One girl, much older than me, liked me very much. She sat next to me the whole night. She brought me sake after sake. We had a long, hard day of work, but now I was relaxing and having a great time. There was so much food and drink. I kept eating and eating and drinking and drinking, pretty soon I could not see if there were beautiful geishas or ugly geishas around me. I could not tell the difference. It was a wonderful time.

The tour was over. It was time to return to Tokyo. I started training again, but I had lost my respect for Rikidozan. One day he came into the gym where I was training with Yoshihara and Yoshino Sato. He wanted to train with me. We got into the ring to wrestle. Rikidozan was 250 pounds; I weighed 190 pounds. I knew how to take care of myself. He tried to beat me, but he could not take me down. He was furious.

Rikidozan said to me, "Kojima, in order to go to the United States, you have to get bigger. You do not weigh enough. Before you become a real professional wrestler, you need to make a name for yourself by being a good sumo wrestler or a judo master." I was adamantly against this idea. I told him, "I do not have to go to a sumo wrestling school to become a famous American style wrestler." At that moment I quit. I said to myself, "Mr. Rikidozan, I promise you. I promise you. I will make myself go to the United States. You will find the name Kojima when you come to the United States." I was determined. Then, my struggle to come to the United States began.

4 ON MY OWN
DREAMING AND TRAINING

I continued my hard training every day on my own. I trained in karate. I trained in judo. I trained in wrestling. I was introduced to Sasahara, the coach of Chuo University. He was a good friend of Yoshihara. In 1956, Sasahara went to the World Olympics, and he won the gold medal for 136 pounds freestyle wrestling. He allowed me to train with his wrestling team at the university. I went to the karate dojo to study judo and karate. I wanted to learn every Japanese martial arts. I was preparing every day for my dream of coming to the United States. My mind was on the United States every day, but it was a very difficult time. The more I trained I became stronger and stronger; however, I was continuously hitting obstacles to leave the country. I was extremely frustrated.

In those days, Japan was a developing country; therefore, ordinary people were not allowed to leave the country. People could not have American dollars, but in order to buy an airline ticket a person needed American dollars. The Japanese yen meant nothing to buy an American ticket. The only way to get American dollars was to go to the Ministry of Finance and fill out an application. They asked, " For what purpose are the dollars needed?" I was a young boy of nineteen years. I said, "I want to go to the United States to wrestle." The workers at the Ministry of Finance laughed at me. "How can Japan benefit from you? Can you send American dollars to Japan?" I had been rejected.

The only way I could get to go to the United States was if I had a sponsor or a promoter invited me, but I did not have any connections. In those days, there were many export companies who said they could get a ticket to the United States so easily. This was bullshit! My emotions were running high; I was overwhelmed with frustration. At times I felt like I was having a nervous breakdown, because I was ready to leave the country but I had no opportunity. I thought about my dream of America. "How can I pursue my dream?" I asked myself over and over. Some days I lost confidence. I told myself, "Kojima, you are not going to make it. Your dream is not going to come true." Then, I would be trapped in a negative gloom. My mother looked at me with pity. She could not help me. I did not want to see anyone. I would pull the futon over me, so no one could see me suffering.

*****

During the days I was still training hard. I had to stay strong. When I was practicing karate, I always did well. But in the gymnasium, I could only practice form. I did not know how hard I could really hit. My close friends and I went to the streets to test out our karate skills. We went to a bad section of the Ginza looking for trouble. It was funny, because there were other young boys out at night looking for trouble, too. We would casually stroll down the street. Then when we passed a group of rough boys, we would bump shoulders with them. I would say, "Oh, I am sorry." Then my friends would say, "Oh, sorry." The rough boys would say, "Boy! Sorry does not help. You have to say it more deeply." I said to them, "I said sorry and that is enough." Then, the rough boys would come at us to attack, but my friends and I were ready. BAM! BAM! BAM! The rough boys would be lying on the ground. We were standing tall, proud of our karate skills.

*****

Tatsuo was my karate teacher. He was a genuine karate teacher from the street. As a young boy, he actually fought in the street with his opponent using a samurai sword. His son and I trained together. There were several styles of karate in Japan. Each was taught in different karate clubs. Sensei Tatsuo told his son and me, "I will take you to challenge the clubs." We went to the clubs and my teacher would say, "Please, I have two disciples. I would like my disciples to test against your disciples." Unfortunately, the karate clubs knew my teacher was a karate master. His reputation preceded him. They would say to him, "Welcome to our club. We cannot accept your challenge, but we would like to sit down with the master. Please look at our training."

*****

Even though I was training every day, keeping my body strong, my heart was in agony. I did not know how I would get to leave the country. There was no solution. My dream was to come to the United States, the land of opportunity. My mother was heartbroken watching me suffer. One day, she told me about her uncle. This was not a real uncle, but a close family friend from the village where she grew up. His family was very intellectual. My mother's uncle went to Alfred University in upstate New York. After he graduated, he followed one of the members of his family to Peru, South America. They bought land to produce cocoa leaves. The cocoa leaves were sent to Japan to make cocaine for anesthesia. His land produced large amounts of cocoa leaves. He was part of the high society, but he also helped out the Japanese immigrants. At that time there were over 70,000 immigrants living in Peru who came there in search of their fortune and then planned to return to Japan.

World War II changed everything. The Peruvian government confiscated the land of my mother's uncle. He lost everything. Plus, there was no longer a high society within to exist. Fortunately, one of the immigrants my mother's uncle had helped earlier remembered the favor and returned it. The immigrant's name was Shirasaka. My mother's uncle lived with Shirasaka and his family. Even though my mother's uncle had lost everything materially, he still was considered to be an honorable man. He had many influential ties in Japan.

My mother told me this story of her uncle. She told me she would write a letter to her uncle, Masao Masata, introducing me. Then, I would write a letter to him explaining my dream. A spark of hope lit in my heart again. I had no idea where Peru was when my mother told me this story, but I found it on a map. I said to myself, "This is the first step. Go to Peru. Once I leave this country, then country to country, I could hope to travel. My dream was alive.

*****

Masao Masata wrote me with a plan of action. I was so excited. He told me to visit Mr. Kesuke Oyama, president of a prominent Japanese business. They met each other in Lima, Peru when Mr. Oyama was there on business one time. I went to the Oyama house. I knocked on the door. The mother answered the door. I showed the letter to her. She smiled and welcomed me into the house. This was the first time I met Kesuke Oyama. I explained my dream to him passionately. He was a man with a big heart. Mr. Oyama liked to see a young boy with a big dream, desiring an adventure. He told me he would do everything he could to help me.

Mr. Oyama graduated from one of the most prestigious private universities in Japan. He knew many alumni who worked in high government positions. He said to me, "Kojima, when you are ready, I will introduce you to the head of each government ministry that you need.

After I met Mr. Oyama, I wrote to my great uncle. I asked him to speak to a promoter in Lima, Peru to give me a contract. He went to Max Aguirre. This promoter did not know who I was of course. He did not know if I could draw a crowd for his wrestling shows. He did not want to gamble a big contract. He offered me a one month contract for little money. I did not care though. As long as I had a contract, this was the invitation to leave the country. My great uncle made the deal with Max Aguirre, and then mailed the contract to me. When I received the contract, I went to Mr. Oyama. I told him I was ready for his help.

Mr. Oyama invited me to his house for dinner. He also invited a few friends he wanted to inspire with my story. Mr. Oyama told them about my big dream of going to the United States. After dinner, he gave me three of his business cards. On the back of each card, he wrote the names of each government official I needed to see, and he told me where to go.

The next day I was so anxious. I walked from my parents' house to Tsurumi Station. I took the train from Tsurumi Station to Shimbashi Station, from Shimbashi Station I walked to where the government buildings were located. I went into the building I needed, and I walked up to the receptionist's desk. My heart was pounding. I showed her one of the business cards that Mr. Oyama gave to me. I remembered the first time I came here when the receptionist laughed at me, then sent me away. However, this time she looked at the card, she smiled, and politely asked me to follow her. She led me to the man whose name was on the back of Mr. Oyama's business card. I do not remember what his name was. I introduced myself to him. He looked at me with a big smile and he said, "Yes, I will help you." I received 163 dollars from finance, the maximum was 500 dollars but I was not allowed this much. My parents did not have much money. I was given my passport. Then, I took my passport and my contract to the Peru Consul where I got my visa to go to Lima, Peru. Now, I needed my airline ticket. My parents gave me the money to buy an airline ticket. I never believed my parents could have had 825 American dollars worth in Japanese yen to buy a ticket for me, but somehow they did. A ticket had to be purchased with American dollars; therefore, Mr. Oyama introduced me to a friend of his who had conducted business with South America for many years. I gave him the Japanese yen for my ticket, and he made the arrangements for me. I was to fly on Canadian Pacific Airlines.

For three years, I struggled to find my way to leave the country. Now this was real. The shock had hit me. Everything I desired was coming true. Anxiety and fear enveloped my mind and heart. I lost my confidence. I thought to myself, "Can I make it?" Big tough Kojima had become a scared little boy. It took almost two weeks to overcome my anxiety. Then, my positive, confident side returned. Like the saying goes, "time solves everything". I was ready when my time came. It was April 13, 1960. It was raining at Haneda Airport. My family and all my friends came to the airport to wish me good luck. A newspaperman even came to record me leaving Japan. I had 163 dollars and a one way ticket to Peru, South America. I told my parents, "If I do not succeed, you will never see me again."

5 FLYING FREE
PERU

My first airplane trip was a long one. Canadian Pacific Airline flew from Tokyo to Vancouver to Mexico and then to Peru. The airplane was called Britannia, a four engine jet prop plane. To fly from Tokyo to Vancouver, the flight took about thirteen hours. I had a four hour layover in Vancouver. Fortunately, I met a Japanese businessman who was flying to Buenos Aires, Argentina. He spoke Spanish and knew much about the culture. We passed the time talking about South America. He helped me during the long journey. From Vancouver we flew to Mexico. I remember flying over the Rocky Mountains, because our plane shook violently. I was scared, but also in awe of the land I could see far below me. However, I did not want to crash into those beautiful mountains. The turbulence ended; we safely arrived in Mexico City. At the airport an agent from the Canadian Pacific Airlines greeted me and the businessman whom I had just met. We had a day to rest before the next flight, so the airline gave each of us a hotel room. The next night our flight left for Lima, Peru. I was getting very anxious to arrive in the new country. When we landed in Lima, I said good-bye to the businessman. He was staying on the flight to Buenos Aires, Argentina. I walked off the airplane, down the stairs to the runway. Waiting to greet me were my great uncle, Mr. Masao Masata, and many of his friends. This was the first time I met my mother's uncle. We took a taxi to where my uncle lived at the Shirasaka family house. The taxi driver's name was Gonzalez who was an old family friend of the Shirasaka family. Everything around me was new. My heart was filled with excitement to begin this adventure.

When we arrived at the Shirasaka house, there were more people waiting to greet me. The people belonged to the Fukushima Province Club. Fukushima Province is where my mother's uncle and the Shirasaka family's father had lived in Japan. The immigrants from the same provinces formed clubs to support and socialize with their own people. I had a big welcome party given by the Fukushima Club at the Shirasaka house. The sons of the Fukushima Club were born in Peru. They had Japanese faces, but they did not speak Japanese. They were born Peruvian. They spoke Spanish, but their parent spoke Japanese. It was very strange for me at first. There were many young boys and girls with their parents waiting to greet me. We had plenty of food and drinks to celebrate. This was the first time I saw so many kinds of fruit. Bananas were expensive in Japan in those days. Ordinary people could not afford them. But when I arrived in Peru, I saw many bananas and other tropical fruits. I was shocked and happy. I had been flying for three days. I was exhausted, buy I was young so I did not really know what tiredness was. I was happy to be in Lima, Peru. To be at the first step for my future success.

*****

The next day, my uncle took me to see Max Aguirre, the wrestling promoter for Lima, Peru. He had made previous arrangements with him. At the office, there was a publicity man waiting for me. He asked me many questions. He took pictures of me to create a poster for the office wall and for the street advertising. I had a week before my first match, so we had to build up the publicity. "Young professional wrestler from Japan, first time in Peru." This was the publicity all over Lima.

The first week passed. The wrestling show was going to be at Luna Park, an outside arena that held about 6000 people. I did not expect too many people to show up for my match. Who knew about me? All the publicity must have worked, because when I arrived in the taxi, so many people were waiting to get into the arena. I did not know if they came to see me or to see the other wrestlers. The taxi driver told me the people were there to see me; usually not many people went to the arena. When I got out of the taxi and walked into the arena, people were yelling, "Kojima! Kojima! Kojima!" I could not believe it! I had a hard time going through the arena to get to my dressing room. I never believed that I would have such a great welcome by the Peruvian wrestling fans.

That night I was extremely nervous. There were almost 6000 fans cheering for me. My opponent, I still remember, was Benito from Argentina. I beat him in about six minutes with a great karate chop. The people went crazy. They had never seen a young Japanese boy so agile and win so fast. I was surprised, because I thought I would have to work in the preliminary match. I waited and waited for my turn to wrestle. I was the last match, the main event. I asked my promoter why I was the last match. He told me, "All the people came to see you wrestle. That is why you carry the responsibility of the last match." I could not believe it. I was a twenty-two year old boy who never wrestled overseas before, and I was the main event in Lima, Peru! It was like a dream. When I won the match, the people were excited. I came out of the ring, and the people carried me on their shoulders all the way to the dressing room.

The promoter, Max Aguirre, was pleased. He did not expect that I would draw that kind of crowd. He came into the dressing room. He shook my hand and said something to me in Spanish. I did not know what he said, because at that time I did not understand one word of Spanish. Then, I took a shower and dressed into my street clothes. When I went out of the dressing room, there were more people waiting to give me congratulations. It was so crowded outside I had a hard time getting a taxi. But, finally I managed to get one, and I went home to the Shirasaka's house. There were many friends waiting for me to arrive so we could have another celebration.

*****

In Lima, Peru I wrestled on Sunday nights and on Thursday nights; therefore, I had plenty of free time except for training during the day. There were many Japanese young people native born in Lima. They were around the same age as me. They had a club called "The Good Morning Club". Many did not speak Japanese at all. They looked like me, but we had to communicate in Spanish. Some spoke Japanese so we got along very well.

The club had a baseball team. It was easy for me to join the team, because I was an experienced baseball player. The Japanese immigration association had their own baseball stadium and every Sunday the club played baseball there. That was their entertainment. Every Sunday we played against the other local Japanese clubs. Then, at night I would go wrestle. It was a wonderful time.

There was a younger Japanese club for the boys fifteen years old or younger. I became the coach of their baseball team. Three times a week I coached the boys. I taught them skills I learned in high school. We played against other young boys' clubs in Lima. My coaching was great, because we won every game. We became the champions of Lima.

I spent my free time visiting friends with my great uncle. One time my uncle took me to a province about 40 miles from Lima. We drove along a two-lane highway with the mountains on one side and the ocean about 200 feet below on the other side. There were no safe guard railings. One mistake, and we would drop off into the ocean. It made me very nervous, but all the drivers seemed confident. They drove in a normal way. We arrived safely at my great uncle's friend's house. It was a farming province. All the Japanese farmers came to meet me. We had a big celebration with Japanese food. My great uncle was so proud of me. I had become quite famous.

The next week we went to my great uncle's step daughter's house. She was an Indian girl whom he had taken in as part of his family, because she had lost her mother and her father. She married a second generation Japanese man who owned a lumber yard. They invited my great uncle and me to their house, and we had a great time. We ate Peruvian food. I loved tasting all the new food and drinks.

Then, the following day, an Italian family invited us to dinner. Their house was way up in the mountains. They had no electricity. I was surprised that in 1960, some people did not have electricity. Oil lamps gave the house light. Our dinner was duck with rice, a Peruvian cuisine. They served their homemade wine with the meal. That was the first time I ever drank homemade wine. We had a wonderful time eating, drinking, and talking.

I had a great life in Lima, Peru. On Thursdays and on Sundays, I wrestled, and then, I spent the rest of my time visiting friends. Every

Saturday night, all the young people, Japanese and Peruvian, got together to have a party with lots of dancing. The party began at midnight and continued into the early morning. All the young ladies had either their mother or grandmother accompany them to the party. The mothers and grandmothers would sit in chairs all night watching the boys and girls dance.

*****

My wrestling name was getting more known every week. My second match went successfully, and my third match in Luna Park was sold out three days before opening. In this match I beat the hero wrestler of Lima. After this match, whenever I was in a public place many people would recognize me. Then, all the newspaper sports sections were writing about me. The first Japanese wrestler to arrive in Lima, Peru making a successful fight, selling out the crowd every time he wrestles. More and more people came to know who I was.

*****

Benito, the wrestler from Argentina, and I became friends. He told me he had two girlfriends from Buenos Aires, girls from his country. He invited me to a movie with them one night. He asked me to meet them. When I arrived, there he was with two girls waiting for me. I will never forget the one girl named Vicki Canton. She was six feet tall with blonde hair. The other girl was Benito's girlfriend. We went to the movie theatre in Miraflores which was a highly respected area. When the movie was over Vicki and I and Benito and Paula were walking the street. Everyone was looking at us. One over six feet tall Japanese man, one blonde woman six feet tall, one man six feet tall 230 pounds, and another very beautiful woman. We were an eye-catching combination. Paula was a dancer in a night club, and Vicki was a commentator at the club. We all had the same schedule. This was the first time I had met a woman with blond hair; I was thrilled. We set up another double date.

For our next date we went to a resort about 50 miles from Lima. We spent the day swimming, eating, and drinking. Then, we came back to Lima for the night life. A few days later, there was a newspaper photo and an article that read, "Kojima is engaged with entertainer Vicki!" I did not know anything about this. My great uncle brought the newspaper to my room, and he asked me what was going on with her. He was angry, because the old Japanese did not want to mix with different blood. He ordered me, "You do not date this girl anymore!" When I was in Japan, I had more freedom, but I had to respect my great uncle and obey his orders. The gossip about Vicki and me was flying through the Japanese community. Because of this, my great uncle ordered me, "Yasuhiro, you are not going out of the house after midnight!" Out of respect I had to obey, "Yes sir." The nightlife of Lima always started after midnight. However, the grandmother of the Shirasaka house felt sorry for me. She whispered to me, "Yasuhiro, when your great uncle is asleep, I will let you go out." She understood I was a young man who wanted to enjoy the night life. She was generous; she always waited for me to come home.

*****

While wrestling in Peru, I met two brothers from Mexico, Salu Montez and Rudy Montez. We became good friends. We became even better friends when I told them I wanted to go to Mexico to wrestle, and then go to the United States. They told me, "When we return to Mexico, when you are ready, we will make arrangements for you to come to Mexico." I was thrilled and grateful, because my heart was in the United States already.

I had been wrestling in Lima for three months when I separated my shoulder. I had to take seven weeks off to recover. I did not want to spend that time being idle. I talked with my great uncle about leaving Lima to go to Mexico. He told my promoter, Max Aguirre, that I would not be able to wrestle for quite a while because of my shoulder injury. Max did not want to lose me. I was the best draw for the shows. Somehow my uncle persuaded Max to terminate my contract. After that I was planning to go to Mexico. My uncle wrote a letter to Salu Montez telling him when I would be leaving Lima for Mexico.

The day arrived for me to say good-bye to all my friends I had met. Everyone came to the airport to say good-bye. My heart was breaking, because I had become close to my friends in that short three months. But my dream for the United States burned strongly within me. I had to push my sadness aside. To my great uncle I said,

"Thank you very much. Without you, I would not be here. I would not be on my way to Mexico." I said good-bye and boarded the plane, bound for Mexico.

6 MEXICO

The trip took about eight hours from Lima, Peru to Mexico City. A plane with only four prop engines did not fly too fast. When I arrived in Mexico City, Salu Montez and his wife met me at the airport. They took me to a hotel called Hotel Foreigners, located near the Arena Mexico where the wrestling office was located. The Arena Mexico held about 22,000 people. It was about a ten minute walk from Hotel Foreigners to the Arena. It was convenient and also a cheap place to stay.

Salu Montez helped me get situated in my hotel, and he told me there was a good restaurant on the corner so I would not have to worry about eating. Then, he left to allow me to get comfortable in my new home. This was my first time in a strange country alone without speaking the language. I did not know Spanish. That was the first day I went to a restaurant and I had no idea how to order. I did not even know what Mexican food was. I got very brave and hungry so I went to the restaurant. They greeted me. Of course I did not understand. They led me to my table and gave me a menu. When I looked at the menu, it was all in Spanish. "How am I going to read this?" I thought to myself. "I do not know how to order anything." I looked around. Then, I pointed to what the people next to me were eating. I said, "Bring me that please." I did not know Mexican food was so hot. When the dish came it looked great, but every time I took a bite my sweat started coming out. I could not believe it. That was my first experience in a strange country eating by myself. After this experience, I became braver. I learned the language a little, so next time I ordered off the menu. Then, the next time I picked out a different dish. Soon, after a week, I knew most Mexican food. Then, I knew how to order what I liked. I did not know how to carry a conversation in Spanish, but I knew how to order food. This was most important to me.

*****

My first night in Mexico City, I had a good night sleep after the long plane flight. Salu Montez came to my hotel the next morning. He took me to the wrestling office at the Arena Mexico to meet the promoter for professional wrestling in Mexico City. He introduced me to the promoter and the booker. They looked at me. They said, "Yes, we could use you. First, we have to get you a working visa. This will take one month." This waiting time was good for me, because my body needed to adjust to the high altitude of Mexico City. It is about 2,600 meters above sea level. In the high elevation I did not have enough oxygen. While my paperwork was processing, I began my training. At the Arena Mexico there was a track at the top. I started running every day, plus did wrestling practice. Then, when my visa was ready; my physical condition was ready.

During my one-month training, I was running and also practicing at the gym. There were many young guys who wanted to become professional wrestlers as well as the established professional wrestlers and the veteran professional wrestlers. There were about 35 guys in the gym all the time. I was the new guy. The gym was the place where I started to learn Spanish. They taught me all the bad words first. I became friends with everybody; somehow they accepted me very well.

One day, Gory Guerrero, a legend in Mexico City, showed up at the gym. He wrestled most of the time in the United States. Arena Mexico was open for ten weeks each year. During this big season, Gory Guerrero returned to wrestle. I was working out at the gym one day, and some boy introduced me to Mr. Gory Guerrero. I said, "How do you do?" He spoke English. I spoke a little English, too. We could carry on a simple conversation. Then, he asked me, "Do you want to wrestle?" I said, " I do not mind, if you want to wrestle, let's go into the ring." All the guys in the gym were looking at the legend, the top wrestler in Mexico against the young boy from Japan. He told me, "Go get your best hold." I said, "You go get your best hold." We came to the middle of the ring. We hung on each other. He tried something, but I countered it. I do not know how I threw, I think I did a Judo throw, but all of a sudden a few moments later, he was on his back on the mat. He could not believe it. "Who can throw me like that?" he shouted. He wanted to try again. The same thing happened. I used another technique, and he was on his back again. He tried five times, then he had enough of me. He quit. We shook hands. He told me, "You are very good." From that point, the other guys in the gym were amazed at how I had thrown their legend. The next morning all the wrestlers in Mexico City knew who I was. I received great respect from all the Mexican wrestlers. They treated me like a Mexican; they treated me very well. I was learning Spanish to carry on a conversation with little difficulty. I had been named "Todo Pistolero" by the Mexican wrestlers. "The Pistol Who Can Shoot Anyone."

*****

Twenty thousand people came to watch my first match at the Arena Mexico. I was to wrestle fifth in the line-up. One main event that night was Copetes Guajardo who was the middle weight champion, and the other main event was Karloff Lagarde who was the welter weight champion. The Mexican wrestlers were not very big. Most were middle or welter weight, only some were heavy weight.

I weighed 195 to 200 pounds, and I stood six feet one inch tall. I was one of the biggest boys. I was not known in Mexico like in Peru. My opponent was Chico Casarez, a little fat Mexican. During the match, when I threw him my head and his head hit. His eyebrow split wide open unfortunately. It took ten stitches to close it up. He was furious. He would not speak to me after the match.

I went into the dressing room, showered, dressed, and waited. I waited until after the last match. Copetes Guajardo finished the last match; then, he came to me and introduced himself. He had heard of my "Pistolero" reputation. He asked me if I had any plans after the show. I had none, just going back to the hotel. He invited me to go out with him.

He had a 1957 Chevy. In 1960, a '57 Chevy was a gorgeous car. Not many Mexicans owned that kind of car, but Guajardo was a top wrestler. He could afford one. He invited me to his house to have something to eat, and then he would drive me home. When we reached his home, his girlfriend was waiting for us with Mexican food. He said, "Let's have a celebration, a welcome to Mexico City!"

We ate a delicious meal. After dinner, he offered me a Mexican drink called tequila. He told me he was going to show me how to drink tequila. "Take half a lime, put salt around the finger, take the shot, suck the lime, lick the salt. First say 'Salud!' Then, drink." We talked for a while, and then we said, "Salud!" Very soon we repeated, "Salud! Salud! Salud!" After eighteen "Saluds!" I did not know where my "Saluds!" were going! I was feeling well acquainted with him. We became close friends. I had a wonderful time at the house of the famous wrestler, Guajardo. He drove me to the hotel. He said, "I will see you tomorrow." I said, "Thank you very much!" I went to my room. I held myself straight until I got to my room. I lied down on my bed in my clothes and relaxed. I noticed the ceiling was spinning around and around and around. The next morning came. I woke up in the same place fully dressed!

*****

The wrestlers working in Mexico City were not given a guarantee. Everyone was paid a percentage of the house. Monday was pay day and booking day. I received the booking sheet of where I was scheduled to wrestle the following week. Fortunately, I always had four or five good bookings every week. I wrestled with all my heart, but the wrestling was only part of my life. In this story, I do not want to describe how I wrestled, if I won or if I lost. Spending time in Mexico was my great experience. Travelling from show to show and living in Mexico is the story I wish to tell.

During one week, Monday my booking was in Oaxaca located south of Mexico City. We had to leave at eight o'clock in the morning from Mexico City, travelling by a two-way road to Oaxaca. Much of the road along the way was only made of dirt. We travelled in a small van with the referee as our driver. It was a long journey from eight o'clock in the morning to six o'clock in the evening. We stopped for lunch and for a few breaks to stretch our legs. I could not believe my eyes! There were people along the road with sombreros, white clothes, and donkeys like I had seen in the movies. In the country side people were still living like old times even though in Mexico City, life was more modern. It was fascinating to me.

We finally arrived in Oaxaca. The promoter had a hotel for us to shower and to change our clothes. Oaxaca was a beautiful city filled with old buildings. There were plazas where people got together to socialize. After we cleaned up, we went to a plaza to eat native food. This was the first time I ate real native food, famous cuisine of Oaxaca like dried beef cooked with scrambled eggs, and queso of Oaxaca, a chewy white cheese. The food was delicious! Later, we wrestled in the show, and then we packed up to travel to the next town. We left immediately after the show at one o'clock in the morning, because the trip from Oaxaca to Veracruz was a long one.

We drove along the old country rode in our small van. I did not know that kind of road even existed anymore. Somehow we made it, safely arriving in Veracruz the next day at two-thirty in the afternoon. During our drive we stopped to have coffee or to play cards, just have a break from the van. At some places on the road, it was only wide enough for one car. There was a 200 to 300 feet drop off on the side of the road. I did not know how our driver stayed on the road. When we arrived in Veracruz we had that day off, because we did not get rest driving through the night. Veracruz, located on the Gulf of Mexico, had a beautiful beach. We relaxed in the sand that evening, listening to the music of Veracruz.

The hotel we stayed at was on Rhino Beach. There was no air conditioning, but the breeze blew nicely through the open windows all day. We were comfortable. We only paid one dollar a day. We had no complaints at all. Our dinner was served on the beach. We ate native food like red snapper caught fresh and cooked anyway we liked it. If I wanted it broiled, they broiled it over the fire, or if I wanted it fried, they fried the fish. We ate a hearty dinner, drank a few cervezas, and a few tequilas. My first experience in Veracruz was a great one.

The following day, Wednesday, we put on the wrestling show. The promoter had his own arena that held about 3,000 people. I wrestled hard, building up a big appetite. After the show, one of the wrestlers told me he would take me to a good restaurant. He said there was a great place at the Veracruz train station that served menudo. I did not know what menudo was. We drank a few beers; then, he told me. Menudo was a cow tripe soup. The first time I tasted it, I did not like the soup. But the more I ate it, I got used to the flavor. I liked it. After dinner we returned to the hotel for a restful night's sleep.

The next morning we had to drive to another town. This was a small town that had not changed in the past 500 years. We wrestled that night. Then, drove all the way back to Mexico City. The highway zig-zagged in some places going up and up and up. When I looked down, I saw tiny cars following us. If our driver made a mistake, we would crash to the street about 500 feet below us. We continued driving up to Mexico City about 2,600 meters above sea level.

On the way to Mexico City, we stopped by a few towns to rest. At about two-thirty in the morning we took a break at a small truck stop. Whatever the native Mexicans ate, I ate. From there we kept driving until we reached close to Mexico City at eight o'clock in the morning. We arrived at an assembly place near Mexico City where we got off the bus, caught a taxi, and went home. I reached my hotel around nine in the morning. I had the rest of the day off. There was enough time to sleep and to enjoy the evening.

*****

I was staying at the Hotel Foreigners. One day I met a second generation Japanese man, a wrestler called Mishima Ota. He weighed 148 pounds. He was the feather weight champion. He spoke beautiful English. He was a well-educated man, graduated from the University of Mexico City. He was also an artist. He introduced me to his many friends. One of his friends owned a photography shop. One was a watch maker. One owned a watch repair shop. I became acquainted with them. I spent my leisure time with my new friends. They were Japanese men who did not speak Japanese. That was funny to me.

*****

While I was living at the Hotel Foreigners, Salu Montez came to me with an invitation. He and his wife had an extra room at their house. He offered for me to stay there and pay rent. Salu Montez was always travelling to the United States or other countries. I would be company for his wife and some extra income for them. She would cook all my meals. This was a good situation for both of us. I accepted his offer. I was fed good home cooking. It was wonderful, because I ate a hearty breakfast, then went to the gym. I was served delicious, authentic food. I had the warm family style living now.

*****

Now, I want to tell you about a different trip. One week we went to Veracruz. The following week we would travel to the other side of Mexico, to Acapulco. We arrived on Wednesday night. We rested during the day on Thursday; we wrestled that night. On the previous Monday and Tuesday, we had wrestled small towns. Then, we drove all day on Wednesday to Acapulco. We left early in the morning on the bus. We travelled through many different towns. I was amazed that this city was completely different from Veracruz, which is a very old city. Acapulco was built for tourists. It was filled with modern buildings. The beach was also different from Veracruz, and there were tourists everywhere.

We stayed in a dinky, cheap hotel. We could not afford to stay in a big, fancy tourist hotel. But, the food was always great. Most tourists went to the fancy restaurants, but we liked to eat at the native, authentic restaurants. The food was delicious and inexpensive. Acapulco had a lively nightlife. After the show, we went to various nightclubs. We knew all the native night spots, and we had a wonderful time.

Friday morning we awoke early to drive back to Mexico City. We arrived home at night, and we rested after our long trip. The Saturday night show during open season at the Arena Mexico was a big event. When it was not open season, we worked shows in small towns around Mexico City.

*****

The second largest city in Mexico is located about 500 miles from Mexico City. It is called Guadalajara. I was sent there to wrestle for two weeks. On Sunday, I wrestled in Guadalajara. On Monday, I wrestled in a city called Leon. Then, the next day the show was in San Luis Potosi. I wrestled in Rio Verde on Wednesday. Then, I returned to Guadalajara.

Guadalajara was different from Mexico City. It was like the old-fashioned Mexico. Mariachis came from Guadalajara. The food was much better and more authentic than the food in Mexico City. The people were friendlier, too. After spending one day in Guadalajara, it became my favorite city. Also, there were more night spots to experience. After the matches, I had many choices of places to go where I could meet people. Outside Guadalajara, the other cities where I wrestled were way out in the fields. It seemed as if the houses and the cities had not changed in about 500 years.

In San Luis Potosi, I went to a restaurant one night. I was so surprised when I discovered the owner was Japanese. We started talking. He told me he and his family were from California. During World War II, they escaped from the internment camp, and they fled to Mexico. San Luis Potosi became their home.

*****

From Guadalajara, I was sent to the west coast of Mexico. We ran Los Mochis, to Ciudad Obregon, all the way to Nogales, just bordering Arizona.

On those trips, we had to take a regular bus like other people. We did not have our small bus. After one of the matches, I was surprised, because a couple of Japanese guys were waiting for me. They were from California. They owned a farm. They were glad to see me, because they had not seen other Japanese people in a long time. I enjoyed the company of my people as well.

The next day we had to go all the way to Ciudad Obregon, on the west coast of Mexico. Once we left the city, we drove through the desert. On the way to Obregon, the bus broke down in the middle of nowhere. It was night time. There was the desert to the right and the ocean to the left. We were stuck in the middle of the desert.

In the morning, the light came out and we walked through the desert. I saw many long cactus and many small cactus. Some Mexican said the cactus flower had a good taste. I tried it. The flower was very sweet.

Somehow the bus company sent a wrecker to fix the bus. We continued our journey to Obregon. Fortunately, we arrived safely.

The wrestlers called the west coast, "the worst place to wrestle". We did not make any money there. At least, I had a 350 pesos guarantee. Ordinary guys got 250 pesos. In those days, though, 350 pesos was not bad, because my living expenses were low.

All the wrestlers wanted to save money. The arena in Obregon had a room where we put extra beds to sleep at night. I went along with the Mexican boys. I could not say I wanted to stay in a hotel, because I wanted to be one of the boys.

The Mexican west coast was the worst, because the population was low. We did not earn much money. However, I was fortunate to see all those different places. The money was not everything. Seeing different places in Mexico, from Nogales, the desert, the west coast, the cactus, the life style, that was interesting to me. The tour gave me many vivid memories. Even though, everyone else hated the tour, it was worthwhile to me. I had a great admiration for the people who lived in those areas.

*****

After we stayed ten days on the west coast, we went back to Mexico City. When we arrived, there was a new booking waiting for everyone. Monday was pay off day. We went to the office at the Arena Mexico. There was a little window. All the wrestlers waited in the room. When my name was called, I went to the little window to pick up my pay. They took the taxes out first, not too much was taken out. Then, they paid in cash.

Near the Arena Mexico, there was a place called Fritz's. This restaurant served good German beer, steak, and native food. That place was the wrestlers' hang-out. On pay day, all the boys were happy. They would spend lots of money on food and drinks. The Mexican wrestlers really enjoyed their lives. We all spent a long time eating and drinking. Then, we went home to rest.

Life was wonderful. I had no responsibilities. No worry about bills. Rent was cheap. Plus, I earned about $130 a week. That was good money. Regular people only made $3 to $5 a day. I could go to restaurants to spend as much as I wanted on food and drinks.

*****

Wrestling in Mexico was the first time I was truly independent. When I was in Lima, Peru I had my uncle or an interpreter with me.

Also, everything was done for me. My friends were Japanese, too. However, in Mexico I had to do everything myself. I had to take care of myself, earn money, pay rent, wash laundry, order food. It gave me a great feeling. I did not need anyone. I was making good money. I could spend whatever I wanted. I felt strong and independent.

My mind was on the United States of America. I was looking for an opportunity to go to the United States, but I was having no luck. Most Mexican wrestlers were a small size, so they did not want to go to the United States. They would not be able to compete with the big American wrestlers.

I had heard of one legend named Rito Romero. He weighed about 200 pounds. He wrestled for a long time in Texas in the Houston territory. He was a top card in Houston, Dallas, San Antonio, Corpus Christi, and Austin. Many Mexican people lived in those cities. He was more famous than Gory Guerrero in the United States.

One day during open season at Arena Mexico, I was walking toward the garage. I went through the garage to enter the gymnasium. A guy drove into the garage in a 1959 convertible white Cadillac. I could not believe it! The guy got out if his car. He was Rito Romero. I introduced myself.

That night we wrestled at the Arena Mexico. I was wrestling, but my mind was preoccupied with the United States. I wanted to finish the match and talk to Rito Romero about wrestling in the United States. I had so many questions. Finally, the match finished. He explained to me about the Houston territory, about how much money the boys made. I was making $120 to $130 a week; the wrestlers in Texas were earning $2000 to $3000 a week. I was amazed. I believed him, because he drove a 1959 Cadillac. It was one year old. The year we were in was 1960.

Rito Romero told me about how they wrestled in the United States. He gave me ideas, but I had more time to think about it. He did not have connections for me. I did not want to ask him. I told myself, "Have patience. The opportunity will come."

*****

When I was wrestling in Mexico, I was the biggest wrestler. I stood six feet and one inch tall. I weighed 192 pounds. Therefore, I did not have many opponents, but the promoter treated me very well. He always kept me on the upper part of the card. I did not wrestle the main event much, because the top wrestlers were middle or welter weight. I did not complain. The promoter made me enough money weekly.

While I was working in Mexico, I talked to the Mexican wrestlers who had been to the United States. I gathered as much information as I could. I asked them many questions about the wrestling style in the United States. The Mexican wrestlers had a smaller build than the American wrestlers. The Mexican wrestlers moved much faster. The American wrestlers worked in a different style. I had seen many American wrestlers in Japan. I developed some idea of how I should wrestle when I go to the United States. I focused on wrestling, earning money, and finding a way to go to the United States. My dream was alive and beating in my heart.

*****

In the meantime, I was sent to Monterey for two weeks. Monterey is in northern Mexico, about four hours from the Texas border. There was a famous food served in Monterey called "cabrito" which means little goat. Cabrito was always available. It was served barbequed. When a cabrito head was ordered, three heads were served on a plate. The brains were eaten on an open tortilla with hot pepper. When I saw this the first time, I thought it was disgusting. But, I had to try it. I used my imagination, not thinking about what I was eating. It tasted good after a few tries. Each place I went I had to taste the local native cuisine.

From Monterey, we traveled to Laredo on the border of the United States. On the way back from Laredo, the customs agents stopped us. I did not know why. The Mexican wrestlers told me the agents had to check for contraband. Some people crossed the border to buy American goods; then, they brought them into Mexico to sell. The Mexican customs agents were waiting to catch them. They knew the wrestlers and the route we worked, so they let us go on to Monterey.

I stayed in Monterey for about two weeks. I wrestled on Sunday in Monterey. Then I worked in different cities a few days during the week. On Sunday night after the show or on my day off, I went to a restaurant called Hardine's. That was the hang-out for all the entertainment people. One evening a guy named Paco Samaripa introduced himself to me. He stood six feet one inch tall and weighed 210 pounds. He said he worked in a nightclub as a singer. I was delighted to meet him. That night I went to see his show. I sat down in the nightclub, had a few drinks, and enjoyed the Mexican music. Then, the final show, Paco Samaripa, came on stage. He had a beautiful voice. He sang all Mexican mariachi songs.

Also during the show, there was a famous dancer named Vicki Veres. She was only in Monterey two weeks. Many people came to see her at the nightclub.

Paco sent a messenger boy to me after the show. He told me that Paco would like to take me to dinner, so please wait for him to come to my table. I waited. All the people left the nightclub. Then, Paco and Vicki came to meet me. He introduced me to Vicki. We went back to Hardine's to have dinner.

When we were talking during dinner, Paco said he wanted to be a professional wrestler. I said, "You sing beautifully, why do you want to become a professional wrestler?" He told me, "When I was a child, I always dreamed of becoming a professional wrestler, but I became a singer instead."

Vicki said she had been to Houston, Texas. She had traveled many places as a dancer. She described life in Houston to us. I told her in the near future I was going to cross the border. I had big dreams about wrestling in the Unites States.

Paco and I became good friends. He told me he was originally from Guadalajara. He invited me to stay at his house with his family if I was ever in Guadalajara again. I promised him that I would see him in the future, but my two weeks in Monterey had come to an end. It was time to return to Mexico City.

*****

I will tell a different story now. Earlier, I told about a Japanese wrestler named Mishima Ota. He introduced me to his friend, Carlos

Takahashi who owned a watch repair shop. Carlos invited me to his house.

He and his family lived just outside of Mexico City. He had married a Mexican woman, and they had two children together. Carlos said to me, "We are going to Xochimilco. I would like you to come with us."

Xochimilco is a city of canals. It was built on an ancient lake in Mexico City. We took a canoe through the canals to see everything. The flowers were beautiful on both sides of the canal. There were authentic remains of Mexican buildings. I had a wonderful time with the Carlos Takahashi family.

*****

One night after a show, a wrestler named Carlos Segura approached me. He weighed 150 pounds, a welter weight wrestler. He was a good friend to me. He asked me what I was doing that night. I did not have any plans. He invited me to go out with him. He said, "Tonight, you come out with me. We will have a great time."

We met at midnight. He picked me up in his car. He told me, "At three o'clock in the morning I have to pick up my girlfriend." I did not mind. We went to a few night spots, had some drinks. Then, we picked up his girlfriend. Carlos said we were going to a party at a friend's house. It was a beautiful house. There were several guys there. One guy came and sat down next to me. He kept moving closer and closer. I moved away. He moved closer. Then, he put his arm around me. Carlos saw him, and winked at me. Suddenly, I realized this guy was trying to be special friends with me. Of course, I was not interested, and I nicely told him so. It was the first time a guy tried to be my date! It was funny to me. I had a good night out with Carlos and his girlfriend.

*****

I had been living in Mexico for eleven months. I experienced many new things. My mind was set on going to the United States to wrestle. However, at the present time, I was getting a good education, meeting different people, and experiencing life.

One day I met a wrestler named Blackie Guzman. He used to wrestle in Houston, Texas. He was the greatest Mexican wrestler in Houston. He became sick and he could not wrestle. The promoter, Morris Sigel, knew what a great card Blackie Guzman was, so he gave him the opportunity to go to Mexico to find new talent. Blackie Guzman was now like a manager.

Blackie Guzman asked me, "Would you like to come to Houston?" I said, "Why not?" I had been dreaming to go to the United States. He told me he would like to fix my visa to go to the United States. We did negotiations. He would receive a percentage of the money I earned. I said, "No problem." All I wanted to do was to get to the United States of America. Once I left Houston, then I would have no obligation to pay him any percentage. Blackie Guzman wanted me to pay him thirty percent after expenses. We made the agreement.

Blackie went back to Houston. Within the next month, he would send my visa. Then, I would go to the American Counsel in Mexico City. They would check out my visa, and then approve it. Once this was done, I would notify him. Then, he would send me the schedule. I was excited. It was happening. I was going to the United States, finally. In the meantime, I continued wrestling in Mexico City.

When my time in Mexico City was nearing an end, the promoter asked me if I would like to go to Ciudad Juarez for two weeks. The promoter in Ciudad Juarez wanted me. I showed him my courtesy, because he had treated me very well. I called Blackie Guzman. I told him I must go to work in Ciudad Juarez for two weeks. Then, I will go to Houston. Blackie agreed.

*****

From Mexico City I took the bus to Ciudad Juarez. The ride took twenty-eight hours. We travelled through the middle of Mexico. The boys told me to stay in a hotel called "Sevilla". When I checked into the hotel, I saw a big sign that said, "Paco Samaripa, tonight at the club". That night I went to see him. I had a few drinks and enjoyed the show. He had such a beautiful voice. I waited for him after the show. When he saw me, he was surprised and happy to see me again.

My contract with the promoter of Ciudad Juarez was that I wrestle only on Sunday night and Wednesday morning. I had plenty of free time to enjoy the exciting new town. It was located close to the border near El Paso, Texas. This city was very busy.

My friend, Paco Samaripa, was working every night at a club. I spent most of my free time with him, going to different night clubs, having a good time my last two weeks in Mexico.

Ciudad Juarez was a bustling city. Many tourists crossed the bridge from El Paso. In those days, the 1960's, there were not many problems. The people were friendly and happy. The city was a safe place.

The two weeks went by quickly. My playtime in Mexico was over. I promised Paco we would see each other again one day. I took the long bus ride back to Mexico City. Then, a few days later, I was on my way to Houston, Texas.

*****

From Mexico City, I flew on Pan American Airline to Houston. On the way to Houston, the plane turned around to return to Mexico City. We did not know what had happened. We landed back in Mexico City safely. The passengers were told the plane had engine problems.

I took a taxi back to my home where I used to live. Mrs. Salu Montez opened the door. Surprised to see me she asked, "What happened to you?" I spent the night, restlessly waiting for the next morning. Finally, the day began, and I started my journey once again. This time the plane took off from Mexico City, and we safely arrived in Houston, Texas as planned.

More than four years of dreaming of America, the Land of Opportunity, filled my heart. Finally, I had arrived. The plane landed. I went through customs and immigration. Blackie Guzman was waiting for me. He picked me up and we drove downtown Houston. My new home was the Milby Hotel. It was a nice old hotel. The wrestling auditorium was only a couple of blocks away. I could walk to the shows. There were many wonderful restaurants to experience also.

Morris Sigel and his brother were the promoters for Houston. The office was in the old building across the street from the Milby

Hotel. After I had checked into the hotel, Blackie Guzman took me to the wrestling office to introduce me to the promoters. I received my booking sheet. My schedule said I start the following Monday.

I never dreamed I would start wrestling right away in the United States. I had struggled such a long time to come to the United States of America. This was my dream. Now, my dream would begin the following Monday! My heart was pounding with excitement!

7 LIVING THE DREAM
WRESTLING IN AMERICA
THE HOUSTON TERRITORY

The circuit in Houston, Texas territory started Monday in Fort Worth, Tuesday in Dallas, Wednesday in San Antonio, Thursday in Corpus Christi, Friday in Houston, Saturday in either Beaumont or in Lake Charles, Louisiana. Sunday was our resting day. This was the schedule.

The following Monday came. Blackie Guzman, a couple other wrestlers, and I drove to Fort Worth. This was my first night wrestling in the United States. This was my first match in the Land of Opportunity. Excitement filled my head and heart. I do not remember the name of my opponent. I climbed into the ring, ready to wrestle. That was the best feeling. My heart was full. I wrestled skillfully.

After the match, we drove to Dallas. We stayed the night at the White Plaza Hotel in downtown. The bill was $4.50.

Then, on Tuesday night I was scheduled to wrestle in a place called The Sportatorium. The show was great. I wrestled, loving every moment of fulfilling my dream. After the show, I heard the story about Duke Keomuka. The Dallas promoter, Ed McLemore, told me about Duke. For 22 weeks straight, Duke Keomuka sold out The Sportatorium. That was amazing. I was not able to meet Duke that night, because he was in Cleveland, Ohio. In a couple weeks he would return.

The next trip on Wednesday was to San Antonio. This town had a real Mexican flavor to it. I felt like I was back in Mexico City. The Mexican people were great wrestling fans. That night at the arena, half of the fans were Mexican. The promoter always featured a top wrestler from Mexico like Rito Romero or Gory Guerrero. That night Rito Romero was wrestling.

I saw Rito Romero in the dressing room. He looked at me and said, "Kojima! Welcome to the United States!" I was very happy to see him. When I met him in Mexico City, I felt like he was a big star, but now I was in the same category in the United States. Rito Romero was the main event. He was wrestling against an American boy. The fans were excited, cheering for Rito. They wanted him to kill his opponent.

We stayed that night in San Antonio after the match. The next day we drove to Corpus Christi. Between Corpus Christi and San Antonio, we drove through the Texas plains. The guys told me if you drive at night you hear the howling of coyotes. The following Monday, I started the same route, going to Fort Worth, to Dallas, to San Antonio, to Corpus Christi, back to Houston.

On Tuesday, in Dallas, I met a guy names Nick Bockwinkel during the daytime. He told me he would show me the tallest building in Dallas. He took me to the building. At that time, it was a tourist attraction. We went all the way to the top. The view was incredible. I could see for miles and miles from the top of that building.

After we finished wrestling the show in Dallas on Tuesday, we stayed overnight. Then, we drove to San Antonio on Wednesday afternoon. After the show that night some boys said, "Let's drive to Corpus Christi tonight instead of spending the night in San Antonio." We ate dinner and took off for Corpus Christi.

It was about 250 miles from San Antonio to Corpus Christi. We were feeling good. We had a few beers. We drove fast, about 100 miles per hour. One boy said, "Hey! Pull over. I will show you something." We pulled over to the side of the road. There was no traffic on the highway. He started howling like a coyote. I did not believe him. I said, "Don't bullshit me!" Then, a couple other boys started howling. All of a sudden, I heard howling coming from all directions. "Wow! This is for real! It's like a western movie!" I said. The boys told me that during the day, sometimes you see dead coyotes hanging from fence posts. The ranchers killed them and hung them up. That was true. The following week I saw five coyotes hanging from the fence posts. When I saw that it was real, I remembered all the western movies I watched as a child in Japan. I never missed a western movie.

*****

One Sunday, Blackie Guzman invited his wrestlers and their friends to his house. I was introduced to everyone. Fortunately, I had learned to speak Spanish during the eleven months I was in Mexico. I had no problem communicating with everybody. I had a great time.

Mario Milano brought his wife and daughter. I still remember vividly his daughter's after dinner entertainment. She spoke poetry. I was amazed at how beautifully she spoke. All the people listened in awe to a ten year old girl. I did not understand all of the poetry she spoke, but the way she spoke was so eloquent and beautiful. I saw that all the people were thinking about it.

We had other entertainment as well. There was festive music. Also, many of the boys sang Mexican songs. We had a wonderful time eating, drinking, talking, and celebrating.

*****

We arrived in Corpus Christi. That town also had many Mexican people living there. Naturally, Rito Romero was the main event. After we finished wrestling, we drove back to Houston for the Friday night show. The auditorium was in downtown.

My promoter made up my wrestling name in Houston. When he received my paper for immigration, it said my name was Saito. I was already "Kojima Saito" when I arrived in Houston. In Peru, I wrestled under my real name, Kojima. In Mexico, my name was Suhiro Kojima. They were all fine names to me.

In the Houston territory, the biggest wrestling towns were Houston and Dallas. Houston drew from 5,000 to 6,000 people. That was big for 1960 and 1961.

Then, on Saturday we went to Beaumont, Texas. This was the first time I saw oil refinery companies. It was interesting to see how the petroleum became gasoline. The whole town smelled like gasoline.

Our day off was on Sunday. In those days, no one wrestled on Sunday. People attended church and rested that day. Blackie Guzman invited me to his house. He wanted me to get acquainted with the boys who were working for him. He had three Mexican boys and a Venezuelan boy working for him under the same situation. I also met Ciclon Negro.

*****

  The third week in the Houston territory, Buddy Rogers was in Houston for a one week tour. He was called Nature Boy Buddy Rogers, the World Heavyweight Champion. I had heard about him when I was in Mexico City. He stood six feet tall. He weighed 245 pounds. He has blond hair and suntanned skin. The way he performed was beautiful. In those days, everyone tried to imitate how he worked in the ring.
  I met Nature Boy Buddy Rogers in Dallas on Tuesday night. He was wrestling against Dory Dixon, a wrestler from Jamaica. It was a good show. I remember Dory Dixon from Mexico City. I had wrestled him at the Arena Mexico. Buddy and Dory drew a large crowd.

*****

  Each week I was following the same routine. I started in Fort Worth. Then, I went to Dallas. One night in Dallas, the main event featured Duke Keomuka and Rito Romero. The place was packed. All the Mexicans wanted to see Rito Romero kill Duke Keomuka. They hated Duke.
  That night was the first time I met Duke Keomuka. I introduced myself to him. I told him in Japanese, "I have heard so much about you. I am pleased to finally meet you." He said, "Please forgive my Japanese. It has been a long time since I have spoken the language. I am pleased to meet you, too."
  Most of the wrestlers stayed at the White Plaza Hotel that only cost $4.50 a night. Duke and I stayed at the Adolfo Hotel. It was a first class hotel. We paid $8 a night. Today, I believe it would cost about $150 to $200 a night.

After the match I usually went to dinner with Blackie Guzman, but Duke asked me if I would like to join him for dinner that night. I asked Blackie if he would mind; he told me it was okay with him. Duke Keomuka against Blackie Guzman was the biggest card in Dallas, San Antonio, and Houston. They were close friends.

*****

The next day Duke asked me, "Would you like to drive to San Antonio with me?" I asked Blackie if he minded. He told me, "You can go with him, because you miss Japanese people. Duke misses Japanese people, too. It will be good for both of you to ride together." We all agreed. Duke picked me up and we took off for San Antonio.

Duke had a green Cadillac, Fleetwood 1960. He told me to put on my seatbelt. "Why do I need to wear my seatbelt?" I asked. I never wore my seatbelt in those days. "You have to wear it," he said. After we got out of the streets of Dallas, the car started accelerating on the highway. I saw the speedometer going to 80, to 90, to 100, to 110. The car was going 110 miles per hour all the way to San Antonio. It was a distance of 250 miles. We took less than three hours to reach San Antonio.

During the car ride, Duke told me his story. He was born in Los Angeles. His father was an immigrant from Kyushu. He was working as a farmer. The time came for him to marry. In those days, the Japanese did not marry for love. The marriages were arranged by the family. Duke's mother came from the same province in Kyushu. She came all the way to Los Angeles with a picture. It was called a picture marriage. His father had a picture of her; his mother had a picture of him. When she got off the boat, they looked at their pictures. That was the way they were married.

Duke grew up on a farm in the Los Angeles area. He could not speak English, because his family spoke Japanese every day. When he enrolled in grammar school and mingled with the American boys, he learned English. Being in school was how he learned his English.

He told me about his experience during World War II. All the Japanese on the west coast were sent to camps, because the United States government thought the Japanese people would rebel against the American people. More than 100,000 Japanese people were gathered and then, they were sent to camps in Montana, Wyoming, or California. Their possessions were confiscated by the government. They were only allowed to take possessions they could carry. They lost everything else to the American government. This is what happened to Duke's family.

Duke spent some time of his young years in the internment camp. Then, in 1943 the American government asked for volunteers for World War II. Duke volunteered for the merchant marines. He was sent to New York for two months of training. Then, he boarded an American transport ship. The ship left out of New York or New Jersey harbor in a convoy. It was protected by a Navy destroyer, but the German u-boats were waiting for the convoy. Some ships were hit, but the convoy continued all the way to England. Duke said, "Fortunately, I survived until the end of the war."

This is the story he told me while driving 110 miles per hour to San Antonio. The time went by like nothing.

*****

That week I traveled with Duke from San Antonio to Corpus Christi and all the way back to Houston. He told me, on Sunday he would introduce his family to me. He would pick me up, and we would have dinner at his house.

So that Sunday, he came to pick me up, and he took me to his house. His wife, Dorothy, was pregnant with their son, Patrick. Duke's mother was there. She came from Los Angeles to help Dorothy during her pregnancy.

We had a wonderful time. It had been a long time since I ate Japanese food. I really enjoyed it. Duke and I became lifelong friends. I knew his children as they grew up. I helped raise them like they were my own children.

*****

The following week Lou Thesz was coming to Texas. Duke told me, "Lou Thesz will be in Dallas. I will invite you and Lou to a nice Italian restaurant. A friend of mine owns the restaurant."

When I became a professional wrestler, I heard the name "Lou Thesz". He became the World Heavyweight Champion at the age of

18 years in 1938. His manager was Ed the Strangler Lewis. Lou Thesz was like the god for all young wrestlers. Also, he came to Japan to wrestle Rikidozan. This was after I had left Rikidozan.

I thought to myself, "Boy! This is Lou Thesz! Someday, I would like to wrestle against him."

Duke told me, "Next Tuesday, I will invite you and Lou Thesz to my friend's restaurant." I could not believe it. I said to myself, "Could this be a dream? I worship Lou Thesz like a god!"

After the match on Tuesday, we were changing in the dressing room. Lou Thesz put on a nice suit and tie. He looked like a real gentleman. He did not look like a wrestler. The only thing that showed he was a wrestler were his two big cauliflower ears. Duke introduced us. He said, "This is Lou Thesz." Lou said to me, "Hey Kojima, nice to meet you." When I shook his hand, I did not know what to say. I never dreamed I would meet the great champion, original wrestler.

We went to the Italian restaurant. Duke introduced us to his friend, the owner. He had prepared a special dinner for us that was not offered on the menu. We were served many home-made Italian dishes. We drank a few bottles of red wine. This was the first time I ate cooked pig feet. We had a wonderful time. The whole night felt like a dream to me.

I thought Lou Thesz would talk to me like I was a little kid, but he spoke to me like a friend. I called him "Mr. Thesz". He told me, "Please, don't call me Mr. Thesz, call me Lou." I said, "Lou, someday I am going to wrestle you." He said, "Kojima, I am awaiting the opportunity."

When I met Lou Thesz, I was 23 years old; he was 44 years old.

*****

Duke Keomuka was the most hated wrestler in Texas. The fans loved to hate him. However, he had many millionaire friends. One friend owned oil drills. One had a transport trucking company. Many important businessmen were his friends.

During the daytime when he was not wrestling, we drove around Dallas visiting his friends. He showed me around Dallas introducing me and his friends. We went to different offices. When we entered the offices Duke was always greeted, "Oh Duke! Welcome! It is good to see you!"

Every Tuesday in Dallas, he stayed at the Adolfo Hotel. The manager was a good friend of Duke's. He took care of Duke. The famous wrester, Duke Keomuka always stayed at his hotel, so they became very good friends.

*****

My reputation was getting bigger every week. My wrestling skills were getting better. The time was going very fast. One week, two weeks, three weeks flew by in a flash. Monday came, then all of a sudden it was Saturday, the end of the week. I had been in the Houston territory for three months working the same route.

It was another Monday night in Fort Worth. I was wrestling against Ciclon Negro. He was Blackie Guzman's boy from Venezuela. We were wrestling for about 50 minutes. At the end of the match, he gave me a big suplex. My toe landed on the mat first. I saw my ankle twist half way. It snapped. I knew it right away when I hit the mat; it was broken. The match was over.

Two wrestling seconds came to help me out of the ring. They carried me to the dressing room. In the dressing room at Fort Worth, there was a big ice chest full of beer. The promoter provides beer for the boys after the match. One of the wrestlers, Sputnik Monroe, was in the dressing room, too. Many of the wrestlers did not like him, but we got along fine. He grabbed me right away, and he put my broken foot into the ice chest. The water was full of ice and beer. I could not stand it! It was freezing cold! So cold it hurt until my foot went numb. That saved my ankle.

I could not continue the tour. I had to return to Houston. I do not know how I did it, but somehow I got a hotel. On Tuesday, Duke came to Houston. He took me to Rice University to see the orthopedic surgeon of their football team. The doctor checked my ankle, took x-rays, and put me in a cast. It was the end of the Houston territory for me.

*****

Wrestlers were self-employed. If a wrestler got a broken leg or arm or any serious injury, the work terminated immediately. There was no compensation. I knew this. I never expected anything from the promoter. When a promoter could benefit from me, then I earned money. If I did not wrestle, I did not expect anything.

Iron Mike was a wrestler I had met in Beaumont, Texas. He was living in the Piccadilly Plaza Apartments. He told me his next door neighbor, Waldo Von Erich was living by himself. He did not have a roommate. Iron Mike suggested I move in with Waldo Von Erich.

I spoke with him, and he thought it was a good idea. He had a two bedroom apartment. His previous roommate, another wrestler, moved to a different territory. I moved into the apartment. The situation was convenient for him and for me.

Iron Mike lived next door with his wife. She always asked me if I needed anything from the grocery store. With Waldo, Mike, and his wife helping me, I had sufficient support. Also, Duke visited me on the weekend to help me.

For almost one month I was living by myself with a cast on my leg spending time in the apartment. It was lonely living. Waldo Von Erich was in town every Thursday night. I had company that night, but the rest of the time I was alone. I was a 23 year old boy with a broken ankle living alone in a two bedroom apartment. I could not go anywhere.

I had saved enough money. I did not have to worry about paying rent or for groceries. I had saved every nickel I could. I had no financial worries. One thing Duke told me, "You know you are finished working in Texas. You can go to another territory, but you are still under your visa with Blackie Guzman. To be clean cut, you should leave the country, and then return under a different visa with another promoter." This was a great idea, because I wanted to keep a good relationship with Blackie Guzman.

In January, Duke would start working in St. Louis, Missouri. He said, "When I get there, I will talk to the promoter. Also, I'll speak to the promoter in Kansas City. They can provide a visa for you."

If I remember correctly, that was around December 15, 1961. I went back to Mexico City. It had been almost four weeks since I broke my ankle. It was still weak and sore, but I could walk. I could not run yet. My ankle needed to heal more and get stronger. It was the perfect time to visit my friends in Mexico.

8 VACATION IN MEXICO

Before I left Texas, I called Mrs. Salu Montez to see if I could stay at her house again. She was delighted to hear from me, and she happily invited me to stay as long as I liked. When I arrived in Mexico City, she was waiting for me at the airport. We took a taxi home. It felt wonderful being back in Mexico.

Paco Samaripa was in Mexico City at that time. He told me when he was finished in Mexico City, he was going back to Guadalajara. He said, "Why don't you come stay in Guadalajara? You are welcome at my house. My family has plenty of room."

I had enough money to fly to Guadalajara instead of taking the bus. Paco welcomed me. He introduced me to his mother and father. I had my own private room. It was like an old-fashioned house, a hacienda. Even if an extra person came into the house, it did not bother anyone. I could come and go as I pleased.

Paco Samaripa was singing in his home town at a night club. The night life in Guadalajara was exciting. There were many places to go. Paco knew many young businessmen and wealthy young men. These young men were the sons of rich fathers. They did not have to work much, so they could hang around the nightclubs. He introduced me to all his friends. I could not believe how many friends Paco had, many wealthy friends. They took me to different places, this nightclub, that nightclub. They did not let me pay for anything. We had a wonderful time playing all night long. We went from place to place. Everywhere we went, the places were crowded with people drinking, dancing, and having a good time. We stayed out until six o'clock in the morning. Then, we went to breakfast.

Two weeks passed. I enjoyed Guadalajara. My vacation gave me great pleasure. I was happy Paco had invited me to his house. It was time to hit the road and go back to the United States. I thanked Paco Samaripa and his friends. Then, I went back to Mexico City to plan my return to the United States.

9 KANSAS CITY
ST. JOSEPH
ST. LOUIS

Back in Mexico City, I stayed a couple of days with Mrs. Salu Montez. I went to the American Counsel to get a tourist visa for the United States. Duke told me, "Fly to Kansas City. One of the guys from the promoter's office will pick you up at the airport. He will drive you to St. Joseph, Missouri. You will stay in St. Jo." That was the arrangement.

When I arrived in Kansas City, like Duke said, the guy was waiting for me. We drove to St. Joseph, Missouri which was about 15 miles from Kansas City. He took me to the St. Francis Hotel.

The next morning, one of the boys from the office came to pick me up. The wrestling office was about five minutes walking distance from the hotel. Since it was my first time in St. Jo, the office had me escorted to its location and welcomed me.

I was introduced to a Greek guy named Gust Karras. He asked, "What name did you use in Texas?" I told him I used my real name, Kojima Saito. He said, "I will tell you a story. When I was wrestling in the early 1930's, I was a middle weight wrestler in west Texas. In those days, west Texas did not use big boys, only middle weight and light weight. I had a friend called Marty Matsuda. He was Japanese, about your size, a middle weight wrestler. Marty Matsuda was excellent at judo, and he became a good American style wrestler. He was a good friend to me. You remind me of him. I would like to use his name in honor of him."

I said, " I do not mind. I am very happy to use his name." My first name, Yasuhiro, was too long. We cut it in half. I became the now famous name, Hiro Matsuda.

*****

Gust called the promoter in Kansas City. He made arrangements for me. A guy named Bob, an older guy, sometimes helped Gust Karras promotions. Gust took me to the immigration office in Kansas City to see Bob. My tourist visa was changed to a working visa.

It took only one week to receive a working visa. I thought I would stay around Kansas City. In St. Louis, there was a big show every other week on Friday. I thought I was going to stay around St. Louis, Iowa, Kansas City area. However, I did not stay long, because the promoter from Oklahoma was looking for some good wrestlers. He called Gust asking for any good talent to be used in Oklahoma.

Oklahoma was a junior heavy weight territory. At that time, I was about 200 pounds; I had a nice physique. The Oklahoma territory was looking for wrestlers like me.

*****

At the St. Francis Hotel, I met two guys, Gino Morero and Stan Stediak. They were around the same age as I was. They were looking for a successful future in wrestling also. Stan, Gino, and I, three young boys, we did not have many wrestling jobs, only three times a week. But, we made enough money to pay the hotel bill and to eat.

Gino was Italian. I could not believe how he could sing. There was a piano bar at the St. Francis. On our days off sometimes we would go to the bar. We had a few beers. Someone was always playing the piano. Gino would go up to the piano, and he would start singing. I looked at him. He looked like a gorilla, but his voice was beautiful.

We did not care that we only had three bookings a week, not a full booking. We had confidence that we would make it big in the future.

*****

A month later, I was ordered to go to Oklahoma. Gino was ordered to go to New York. Stan was booked for bigger jobs in the St. Louis area.

February 27 was the last time I wrestled in St. Louis. I was the third match. Duke was wrestling against Paolo Conan, the World Heavyweight Champion. After the match was over, I stayed in St. Louis that night. I said good-bye to Duke. The next day, I took the train to Tulsa, Oklahoma.

10 OKLAHOMA

When I arrived by train in Tulsa, someone was supposed to be waiting for me. I did not know who would be waiting. Jack Gotch came to pick me up. He was a referee. He saw a big Japanese boy get off the train. He came up and introduced himself. He said, "My name is Jack Gotch, the referee for Leroy McGuirk." Later on, Jack and I became good friends. He took me downtown to the office to introduce me to the promoter, Leroy McGuirk. After that, he took me to the hotel.

Jack Gotch graduated from Oklahoma State University. He was the NCAA 124 pound champion two years in a row in the early 1930's. Leroy McGuirk was the 190 pound NCAA champion from Oklahoma State. I do not know the year. Leroy was blind. When he was born, he lost eyesight in one eye. Later, in a car accident, he lost sight in the other eye.

Oklahoma territory was famous with amateur wrestling. College wrestling from Oklahoma State University and the University of Oklahoma was popular. Another guy, Tony Martin, was the sheriff of Tulsa. He was a 124 pound college champion, too. He went to Oklahoma State. Tony Martin was the Deputy Sheriff. He was also the time keeper for the Monday night show. His son, Mickey Martin, went to Oklahoma State University. He was also the 124 pound NCAA champion in 1960 and 1961. The father and the son were both champions.

*****

This was the schedule I followed in the Oklahoma territory. Monday night, I wrestled in Tulsa, Oklahoma. Tuesday, I wrestled in Little Rock, Arkansas. Wednesday night, the show was in Springfield,

Missouri. Thursday, I went to Wichita Falls, Texas. Friday night, I wrestled in Oklahoma City. Then Saturday, I wrestled for television. Sunday, all the wrestlers were off.

The Monday night show was at the Cimarron Arena in Tulsa. It held about 2500 people, and the wrestling office was located there. They introduced me for the first time in Tulsa. I was working to establish myself. After the match, I went back to my hotel for the night. The next morning we were going to Little Rock, Arkansas.

I rode with different wrestlers each time. They picked me up from the hotel. We had a wonderful time driving to the different cities. We drove through cotton fields. The land was different from Texas.

We arrived in Little Rock around six o'clock in the evening. We checked into our hotel, the Lafayette in downtown Little Rock. We had time to relax, because the show did not start until eight-thirty. We went to the arena around seven-thirty. After the match, we drove across the river to a restaurant for dinner. The other wrestlers introduced me to all the places the boys liked to go.

On Wednesday afternoon, we drove to Springfield, Missouri. It was about 215 miles, going through the mountains. We drove along a curvy, two-lane highway. We arrived in Springfield at about six o'clock. We wrestled that night, and after the show, we went back to Tulsa. We did not have to stay in a hotel.

From Springfield to Tulsa, it was about 220 miles. We arrived at three o'clock in the morning. Everyone went home to rest. The next day, Thursday, we went to Wichita Falls, Texas. The drive was about 250 miles. We left at one o'clock in the afternoon. From Oklahoma to Texas, the land was completely flat. There were no trees. I saw only ranches and cattle. We drove faster than usual. It only took five hours to get to Wichita Falls. After the match, we drove back to Tulsa.

On Friday, the show was in Oklahoma City. From Tulsa, it was a 90 mile drive to Oklahoma City. We had plenty of time. We drove the turnpike, a four-lane highway. It did not take a long time to get there. After the match, we drove back to Tulsa. Then, on Saturday, we wrestled for television. On Sunday, we rested. It was the day off for all wrestlers.

This schedule was a big change from my schedule in St. Joseph, Missouri. I only wrestled three times a week there, but when I arrived in Tulsa I had a busy schedule. I did not mind, because I was making great money. Every night I was paid cash. Plus, I was gaining great experience wrestling in the American style.

In those days, the wrestlers were paid cash in accordance with the house. If a wrestler drew a good house, then he was paid a percentage. Every wrestler was competing to be at the top. Naturally, I had so much confidence. When I was in St. Jo, I knew I was going to make money. I felt my great future was very near. It did not take long. In about three weeks, I began to draw a crowd. The people hated me, because I was beating up the American boys, all their heroes. The more the people hated me, the more tickets I sold.

After four weeks working in the Oklahoma territory, I had established myself. The promoter, Leroy McGuirk, saw I had the drawing power. He started booking me as the main event; there was no competition. I kept my main event until I left the Oklahoma territory. I stayed in Oklahoma territory from February 28, 1962 until December 15, 1962.

*****

While I was in the Oklahoma territory, I met a wrestler named Joe McCarthy from Tiger Tail, Tennessee. He had been stationed in Japan during the American Occupation time. He had many memories of his time in Japan. He began telling me stories about what he had enjoyed during his stay. We became close friends.

Joe McCarthy was married, but he and his wife did not have children. They owned a pitbull named Booger Baby. Joe took that dog everywhere, like it was his child. It was a well-behaved dog. Every command Joe said, he obeyed.

Joe told me one day, "Sunday, you come to my apartment. I'll fix you some real southern food." I had no idea what southern food was. On Sunday, I went to his place. He had cooked corn bread, bean soup, turnip greens, fried chicken, and biscuits. I could not believe all the food. Joe said to me, "This is real southern food." I ate everything. The flavors were different than anything I had ever tasted. The food was absolutely delicious.

*****

The wrestlers had another route to work sometimes. It was a long trip, and we did not make much money. All the wrestlers had to work the route, even the top boys, because it was part of the Louisiana territory. The Oklahoma and the Louisiana territory worked together sometimes. The highlight of the trip was a night out in New Orleans. All the wrestlers looked forward to this. At least, we made enough money to enjoy the town.

On Monday, we drove from Tulsa, Oklahoma to Shreveport, Louisiana, about 350 miles. We wrestled in Shreveport that night. After the match, we went to Monroe, Louisiana for the Tuesday night show. We wrestled in a large skating rink. The place held about 1,000 people. The amount of money we could earn was limited, but it was enough for me. Even after I paid my hotel bill, I had plenty of money left.

In New Orleans on Wednesday night, we made good money. The money was nice, but what the wrestlers really loved was the nightlife of New Orleans after the show. We went to Bourbon Street, and we spent all night there. We went to every bar. Pat O'Brien's was a favorite, because of the Hurricane drink they served. Most of the owners knew the wrestlers. New Orleans was a great place to enjoy. I loved the jazz music and the Cajun food.

There was a trumpet player named Al Hart. He had his own bar. He was famous. When he was not on tour, he played at his bar. I used to go to his place. I always had a great time. Another favorite place of mine was the Felix's Restaurant, just at the entrance of Bourbon Street. They served Cajun food with a specialty in raw oysters. There was a raw oyster bar. The bar had no chairs. There were always about fifty people standing at the bar. I stood at the bar, drank a few beers, and ordered oysters. I used to eat about six dozen raw oysters. Then, I ordered seafood gumbo. The bartender opened the oysters in front of the customers. They were served with ketchup and hot sauce, but I liked them with just a squeeze of lemon. The oysters were salty so the sour lemon added a light, delicious flavor. The best oysters came from around the New Orleans area. The Mississippi Delta produced beautiful oysters.

Another New Orleans cuisine I learned to eat was crawfish. They looked like little lobsters to me. They were served whole, from head to tail. I was taught how to eat the crawfish. First, you cracked the middle and sucked the head. Then, you opened the tail. You used your fingers to push the meat out of the shell for you to eat. I was used to eating food like this in Japan. It was not strange to me. The taste was different, but I enjoyed eating crawfish.

New Orleans was my favorite city. The food was delicious, and the atmosphere was good. I had a wonderful time on Bourbon Street every time we wrestled in New Orleans.

After our fun time in New Orleans, we were tired. We just had to get through the rest of the week, but all the wrestlers were in good spirits because they had a great time in New Orleans. On Thursday, we wrestled in a small town outside of New Orleans. After the match, we left at one o'clock in the morning, and we drove 620 miles back to Oklahoma City. We wrestled in Oklahoma City on Friday night. On Saturday, we worked for Oklahoma City television. That was our schedule.

*****

One of the top wrestlers in the Oklahoma territory was Danny Hodge. He had attended Oklahoma State University. He was the NCAA champion of 191 pounds for three years in a row. He was never defeated in college. Also, he went to the Olympics in 1952, the Helsinki Olympics. At that time, he was 19 years old, a senior in high school. Then, in 1956, he went to the Melbourne Olympics where he won a silver medal. Actually, he should have won first place; there was a controversy. A Bulgarian judge gave the gold medal to the Bulgarian wrestler. The decision was made. Danny did not complain. The judges from the Western side said Danny won, but the decision was set.

Danny Hodge was also the Golden Gloves Boxing Champion. He was famous in Oklahoma. He was known where ever he went. College wrestling was very popular in Oklahoma. After his Olympic career, he decided to become a professional wrestler. Danny Hodge was a hero to the people of Oklahoma. The people hated me. They did not want to see me beat their hero. A match between Danny and me would be a big show. We would sell out, which was great for both Danny and me. The promoter knew this, and he wanted to create even more anticipation for the match, Danny Hodge against Hiro Matsuda.

There were other top wrestlers working the main event. I wrestled with them before I met Danny Hodge in the ring. I was building my reputation more and more. People began wondering when Hiro Matsuda would wrestle against Danny Hodge. I was getting more popular; that meant people hated me even more. When the wrestling fans hated me I felt so happy, because my pay-off was getting better and better.

One week in Tulsa, Oklahoma, I wrestled the main event and I won. Some fans yelled to me, "When are you going to wrestle Danny Hodge?" I said, "I will wrestle Danny Hodge anytime. I will beat him!" They yelled, "No way! You're not going to beat the hero Danny Hodge!" I told them, "Hey! Who do you think you are? I came here to build my reputation! I am the best wrestler in Japan! I can beat anyone!" The fans were steaming mad, furious that I was so confident.

Before a match, I climbed into the ring and I walked the perimeter. I looked at all the people. They saw my face and they started calling me names. Then, I smiled big. I shouted, "Where is Danny Hodge? He is hiding from me!" The people were infuriated. The more sarcastic I spoke, the angrier the fans became.

Danny Hodge and I had business to take care of in the ring. We had to build up our reputations and keep the fans anticipating our battle. We wanted to sell out our shows, so we would have a big pay-off. Inside the ring, we were enemies; however, outside of the ring we were gentlemen. We were friends.

*****

I was settling into my life in Oklahoma, especially in Tulsa. I stayed at the Hotel Brigg. There was a nice bar downstairs. They played country music at this bar. A friend of mine introduced the owner of the bar to me. That bar became my hangout place after the Monday night match. The owner and I became good friends. The place closed around two-thirty in the morning. One night he said, "Hiro, let's go across town. I have a friend who owns an after-hours bar." We went to the bar, had a few drinks. We had a great time.

The country bar at the hotel was a popular place. There was a big jukebox, a dancehall, and a long bar. If you wanted to hear good music, you put the coins in the box. Everyone had fun. They served beer, wine, and liquor. I heard many good old country music singers. It was enjoyable leisure time for me.

After having a good time at the bar, it was time to go out for breakfast. The wrestlers liked a place called the Bishop Restaurant in downtown Tulsa. It was open all night, so we could eat breakfast anytime. That was our routine. Wrestle the match, have a few drinks, eat a good breakfast, go to bed. We rested for the next day.

*****

The next day we drove to Little Rock, Arkansas. We left around twelve o'clock in the afternoon. On the way to Little Rock, just before we hit Fort Smith, there was a boring little town. I don't even remember the name of it. However, this town served the best catfish. I tasted catfish for the first time. The pieces were finger size, about six inches, covered with cornmeal, and deep fried. Every Tuesday we stopped in this town to eat. We ate the fried catfish with cornbread. Sometimes they also served buttermilk. I did not like milk, so usually I drank beer. It was delicious. After we filled our stomachs, we headed to Little Rock.

The arena was in downtown Little Rock. It held about 2,000 people. The show started at eight-thirty that night. My name was becoming well known. I remember, always there were the same four girls sitting ringside. They were sophisticated looking girls, but when I got into the ring, they made all kinds of such ugly faces. I walked by them and I said, "Beautiful girls, why do you make such ugly faces?" I smiled big at them. They would get so mad. I just laughed. It was very funny to me.

I wrestled the main event. I was beating all my opponents. My reputation kept growing stronger. The people hated me even more each week. Danny Hodge usually wrestled the same show. He wrestled someone below me. Danny Hodge used to work the main event all the time. Now, we shared the top position. The wrestling fans wanted Danny Hodge against Hiro Matsuda in the ring. At the end of the match, I yelled at the fans, "Don't worry! The time is coming when I will beat your hero, Danny Hodge!"

After the match was over, there was not much to do for entertainment in Little Rock. We crossed over the bridge to have dinner at a restaurant. It was not anything spectacular. We filled our stomachs, and we went to our hotel to rest for the next day.

*****

We left the next day, Wednesday, at twelve o'clock noon. We drove through the mountains, climbing up and up. Then, the road curved down the mountains. It was not an easy drive. I did not have my own car. I rode with different wrestlers. I was at the mercy of their driving skills. Fortunately, we always arrived safely in Springfield, Missouri.

We wrestled that night. After the match, we drove back to Tulsa, Oklahoma. On the way to Tulsa, we stopped in Joplin, Missouri to buy cases of beer, because the alcohol content of beer was 5%. In Oklahoma, the beer had an alcohol content of only 3.2%. Drinking beer with a 3.2% alcohol content was like drinking water. We bought the beer to bring back with us to Tulsa. In those days, Coors was popular in Oklahoma and Missouri, so that was my favorite beer. Also, I enjoyed drinking Budweiser. Both American beers. I liked that.

*****

On Thursday, we drove to Wichita Falls, Texas. After we passed Oklahoma City, just before we crossed the Red River to Texas, there was a small restaurant. It was a mom and pop's barbeque joint. The wrestlers knew it was a great place. The old man and old woman cooked a tremendous barbeque. They made barbeque ribs or sliced beef barbeque. It was served with black beans. We ate a Texas style meal.

In those days, all the wrestlers knew where to stop for a good place to eat. Sometimes, it was a hole in the wall, not many people knew about, except for the local people. Those places served the best food full of flavor. That was part of our enjoyment driving from city to city. We stopped along the way to eat at our favorite places. We became regulars at many places. The people knew us and always welcomed us.

*****

Oklahoma City on Friday night was the largest city where we could make the most money. We wrestled in the Stockyard. Cows and horses were sold in the Stockyard, but it was a nice arena. After the match was over, we drove back to Tulsa. But before we left Oklahoma City, we ate dinner at a place called the Split Pea. It was a hamburger restaurant, and they sure made delicious hamburgers with a special sauce. The place was a hangout for the students from University of Oklahoma. It was always packed with college kids. We would order a couple hamburgers each to take with us on the road. We ate them along the way.

The good thing about the Oklahoma wrestling fans was that most were respectful of the wrestlers. The people hated me when I was in the ring, but outside of the ring, they treated me like a gentleman. Like when I was at the Split Pea, the college boys and girls came to me asking for my autograph. I was just a little older than they were, so they felt comfortable talking to me. I never felt threatened by the fans.

*****

During my stay in Oklahoma, I met a guy named Dick Bailey. He had graduated from Oklahoma State University. He was a two year in a row NCAA 165 pound college wrestling champion. He went to the 1956 Melbourne Olympics. Unfortunately, when he was in Melbourne, he had to have his appendix taken out. He could not compete.

Now, he was a wrestling promoter for a small town in Oklahoma. He ran a spot show once or twice a week. That was how we met. He was still in great shape, and he could wrestle strongly. He asked me, "Do you want to wrestle?" Once in a while, we met at the arena in Tulsa on Sunday morning. Just he and I would wrestle in the arena. We used to fool around about who was the best. I told him, "I did not go to the Olympics, but I can still beat you." We used to wrestle twice a month on Sunday, just for fun.

*****

Leroy McGuirk, the promoter, had a ranch in Tulsa. He owned about 400 cattle. He had a foreman to take care of the cattle. One day he asked me, "Hiro, would you like to come to my ranch? My wife and I will come pick you up." He invited a few other wrestlers, too. They had cars, so they drove to his ranch.

I was very excited. I loved American western movies. I never missed one when I was growing up in Japan. Before I went to the ranch, I prepared for the occasion. I bought jeans, boots, and a cowboy hat. Some of the wrestlers brought guns. We were set. The ranch was about 60 miles from Tulsa. When we arrived at the ranch the foreman welcomed us.

Joe McCarthy, the wrestler from Tiger Tail, Tennessee came to the ranch, also. He was my good friend who had told me stories about being stationed in Japan during the American Occupation. He grew up on a farm in Tiger Tail, and he knew how to handle a horse. Leroy owned a few horses. He asked, "Hiro, would you like to ride a horse?" I said, "I have never ridden a horse in my life." Joe McCarthy told me, "Don't worry about it. I will teach you." He held the horse, and he helped me into the saddle. Joe reassured me that the horse was gentle. He made sure the horse walked slowly. I was afraid the horse would throw me off. Joe took a picture. After riding the horse, I got off and I tried pulling pistols from the holster. I felt like a real cowboy. The other wrestlers rode horses, too. We were having a great time, cowboy style.

The foreman of the ranch cooked a barbeque for us. He grilled hamburgers and hot dogs. We drank a few beers. Then, target practice started. Joe asked me, "Have you ever shot a pistol?" I replied, "No, in Japan guns are prohibited." The wrestlers brought their pistols. We arranged the beer cans for targets, and we started shooting. Joe was a good shooter. I tried to shoot a pistol. I was nervous. Joe told me, "Don't worry. Just squeeze the trigger. Don't pull. Just squeeze." I squeezed the trigger, but I did not hit a target.

Later, Joe started riding a horse. He rode the horse in a real professional style. I was surprised he was such a graceful rider. He was showing off. He would ride fast, then cut sharp, then ride and stop quickly. After a while, I don't know how it happened to the horse, but when Joe stopped, they lost their balance. The horse fell over on Joe onto his right leg. Somehow, he got up. He pulled his jeans down to check his leg. His right thigh was completely blue. Luckily, he did not break any bones. Joe said, "This is not the first time. I have experienced a fall like that before." It did not bother him. I said, " I sure can't afford to take a chance like that; I have to make money tomorrow!" It was nice to ride a horse, but I was not really comfortable. That was my first experience becoming a cowboy.

*****

Another Sunday, Leroy invited me to his house for dinner. He told me he also invited Strangler Lewis. He asked me if I had ever heard of Strangler Lewis. Of course, I had heard of him. Around 1920, he was the World Heavyweight Champion. He lived in Tulsa, now. Leroy and Strangler Lewis were good friends. He said, "When you come to my house on Sunday, you can talk to the old timer."

On Sunday, I went to Leroy's house. He introduced me to Strangler Lewis and his wife. Strangler Lewis was almost blind from glaucoma. I told him I read about him when I was growing up in Japan. He was the World Heavyweight Champion when I was young. He started to tell me stories about the 1920's and early 1930's. He said in those days, there was no income tax. He made over five million dollars. That was an incredible amount of money back then, but he did not save any money. He spent all the money he made. He spent money on women and having a good time. He said he wrestled in front of 15,000 people at some places. He would wrestle a match for one and a half hours sometimes. His best hold was the headlock. That was how he got his name, Strangler Ed Lewis.

It was an honor to meet such a legend of wrestling. He told me many stories of wrestling in his day. He told me about how the business worked and about all the top wrestlers of that time. I enjoyed listening to him, and learning some history of the wrestling business.

*****

Sometimes after the show in Shreveport on Monday night, instead of going to Monroe and then New Orleans, I was demanded back in Little Rock, Arkansas. After the match, I got a ride with other wrestlers. The drive was only about 200 miles; it was not bad.

One night, I was riding with a few wrestlers. There were two guys in the front, and in the back, the referee Jack Gotch and I sat.

We picked up a six pack of beer and Jack bought a pint of bourbon. That was Jack's favorite. After drinking six beers, I was feeling good. Jack finished about three quarters of his pint. We were driving through a wooded area. At night there was not much traffic. Sometimes we saw deer, raccoons, or other dead animals by the road. This night, we saw something big running in the middle of the road in front of the car. I said, "Stop the car! Stop the car!"

They stopped the car. The headlights showed a big cow in front of us. I told Jack, "I am going to catch the cow." I ran after the cow, but the cow ran very fast. The car was following behind me. I don't know how far I ran. I was having a good time, but I could not catch the cow. Finally, Jack yelled, "Hiro! Get in the car! There's no way you can catch that cow!" I gave up and got back in the car. We drove passed the cow. Jack told me, "Take it easy. Drink some bourbon." I drank a couple of gulps, and I thought the bottle was empty. I threw it out the window. Jack screamed, "No! No! No! The bottle's not empty!" But, the bottle was already flying through the air. Jack was so mad and disgusted with me, but I was having a good time. I laughed and laughed and laughed.

We stopped by a small town. In those days, driving through a small town, we only saw a few houses. There usually was only one grocery store and one liquor store. We stopped at the liquor store. I bought another six pack of beer and a bottle of bourbon for Jack. We continued heading to Little Rock.

*****

Danny Hodge was the World Junior Heavyweight Champion at that time in 1962. In those days, the World Heavyweight Champion was Pat O'Conner. He beat Buddy Rogers in Chicago about two weeks before he came to Oklahoma.

The wrestling fans were still waiting to see Danny and I wrestle. They had to keep waiting. The promoter thought I would be a big draw wrestling against the Heavyweight Champion, Pat O'Conner, in Tulsa, Oklahoma. The place was jam-packed. We did nip and tuck for 60 minutes. We had a draw.

I was feeling even more confident. My credentials were stronger now. People wanted to see Danny Hodge against Hiro Matsuda more than ever now. Who would have expected this Hiro

Matsuda to draw after 60 minutes wrestling the World Heavyweight Champion?

Finally, Danny Hodge and I were scheduled to meet at Middle Square Circle. The promoter did not want to do one against one yet. They put us in a tag match. The promoter wanted to give the fans a taste of us wrestling against each other, but continue to build up the rivalry. Danny and I wrestled just enough to tease the audience. We did the tag match for three weeks in a row at different places. Don Kent was always my partner. Danny had a different partner each time. Then, finally, we were scheduled to wrestle alone. Hiro Matsuda meets Danny Hodge in Oklahoma City.

The place was sold out, about 6,000 people. All the crazy fans wanted to see Danny Hodge beat my ass. Danny Hodge had a second who was his buddy. I asked Don Kent to be my second. A second stays in his wrestler's corner in the ring. He watches and makes sure nothing happens outside the ring. The second protects his wrestler while he is working in the ring.

We wrestled for 60 minutes. The fans were excited. The crowd was going crazy, yelling, "Danny! Danny! Danny!" No one was yelling, "Hiro! Hiro! Hiro!" All the fans were chanting for Danny. After 35 minutes of nip and tuck, I tried to pin him. The crowd was hushed silent. Then, Danny kicked out, and the fans went wild. They screamed and cheered.

Danny hit me somehow. I flew across the ring landing near the ropes. One leg was on the rope. Danny pinned me down. The referee started counting, "One, two..." But, Don Kent told the ref, "Look at his foot! It's on the ropes!" The ref realized and stopped counting. He made Danny separate from me, so I could get up. Danny got so hot with anger, he punched Don Kent!

Enraged, Don Kent climbed into the ring and jumped Danny. Don Kent and I beat the hell out of Danny. Danny's second couldn't even help him. While this was happening, I saw some wrestling fans start crawling into the ring. I was chopping one guy, then hitting another guy. Even Danny was hitting right and left at the wrestling fans. One fan tackled me. I put him in a waist lock. I picked him up onto my shoulders, and threw him over the top rope. There were other fans waiting to catch him.

Since the referee lost control of the match, there was no decision. There was no way we could finish the match. The police showed up. They climbed into the ring, and they tried to calm down everyone. The match was over. Another day would come for Danny Hodge against Hiro Matsuda.

*****

One of the top wrestlers working the Oklahoma territory in those days was called Tiny Smith. Later, he became known as The Kentuckian. He stood six feet and eight inches tall. He weighed 330 pounds. He looked like a hillbilly. He also worked the main event in some of the cities. When The Kentuckian was finished with the Oklahoma territory, he went to Florida.

The promoter of Florida was Cowboy Luttrall. The Kentuckian told Cowboy Luttrall, "There is a wrestler named Hiro Matsuda in Oklahoma. He is a big card and he draws a large crowd." Cowboy Luttrall was interested in bringing me to Florida to wrestle. This was how I had the opportunity to come to Florida.

*****

During the hot summer nights in 1962, there were some spot shows once or twice a year. The show was way up in the mountains in Arkansas. Only four or five wrestlers were used for the show. The people in the small mountain town about 220 miles from Tulsa saw wrestling once or twice a year. The show was in a high school gymnasium that held about 3,000 people.

Tiny Smith and I were wrestling each other. We wrestled for 45 minutes in the hot summer night. After the match, we were completely dehydrated. My enjoyment after a match was drinking a cold beer, especially after a match in the summer heat. I asked where we could buy a six pack of beer. To my surprise, we were in a dry county. We could not buy alcohol. I was disgusted.

I said, "We have to drive fast to the Arkansas border!"

Finally, we came to Fort Smith, but it was after one o'clock in the morning. All the liquor stores were closed. I had to quench my thirst with soda pop.

Between Fort Smith and Tulsa, about 50 miles before Tulsa, there was a town called Muskogee. The boys knew about a great barbecue place. They served delicious spare ribs. The owner knew all the wrestlers. He told us not to worry about the after-hours; he would serve us beer anyway. We ate barbeque spare ribs and drank beer. It tasted so good. I was satisfied.

*****

One day after a match in downtown Tulsa, Oklahoma, I was having breakfast in the Bishop Restaurant. A distinguished gentleman introduced himself to me and he asked, "Are you Hiro Matsuda?" I replied, "Yes, I am." Then, he told me, "I am a photographer. I would like to use you as a model, if you do not mind." I agreed. We made arrangements. I went to his studio. He took a few portraits of me.

A large picture of me was shown in the First National Bank of Tulsa. I still have a copy of this picture. I did not even know it was showing. One of the wrestlers told me. He said, "Hey Hiro, there is a big picture of you on display at the First National Bank of Tulsa." I thought he was joking. Later, I found out that the gentleman I had met was a well-known, great photographer.

*****

During my stay in Tulsa, I met a man named Heime Viner. He was a Jewish man who owned a battery shop. Once in a while, he came to the arena in Tulsa. He was a special time keeper for the matches.

He came to me one day. He said, "Hiro, instead of living in the hotel, why don't you stay in one of my apartments?" He owned three apartments above his battery shop. I went to see the place. It was a nice apartment. There were two bedrooms, two bathrooms, a living room, and a kitchen. I decided to move into the apartment. I asked Don Kent if he would like to be my roommate. He thought it was a good situation, so he agreed. It was convenient for the both of us.

Heime Viner took care of Don Kent and me. He was like a father. If we needed anything, he was always there. He had a good business rebuilding batteries. He had several employees, and he was always busy.

Living in an apartment was completely different than living in a hotel. We cooked many meals at home. On Sunday, a relaxing day, instead of staying by myself at the hotel, Don Kent and I spent the day together. Sometimes he cooked; sometimes I cooked. We drank a few beers. Other wrestlers would stop to visit us. Heime came over. Sunday evening was like our family night.

*****

I wrestled Danny Hodge in different cities, but the biggest match the fans were awaiting was in Oklahoma City. The Florida territory had sent a message to me. They told me that when I was finished wrestling in the Oklahoma territory, I was welcome in the Florida territory. I talked to Cowboy Luttrall, the promoter for Florida. I told him I had a commitment to wrestle Danny Hodge in Oklahoma City. When I was finished with that, then I could give notice. I would be ready to go to Florida.

In the meantime, Danny Hodge and I were preparing for the biggest brawl in Oklahoma City. This would be our second meeting in that city. The place was packed, sold out. This match was the winner-take-all. We wrestled for 45 minutes. I wrestled the best I could, but somehow he beat me. I was satisfied though. We met in the ring, straight-forward, man to man. I had no complaints about the match. I gained more experience. I told Danny, "One day, I will beat you."

The fans were afraid I would win. I used to say to the fans, "I will beat Danny Hodge. You people will never see the belt again. I am taking it to Japan, and I am not coming back to the United States." The people were happy I did not win.

*****

One month before I left Oklahoma, I bought my first car. Jack Gotch, the referee, also worked as a used car salesman. He told me, "Hiro, I have a good car for you. It is a 1959 Dodge." He took me to the car lot. I test drove the car. It was beautiful. I bought my first American car.

I did not have a driver's license yet. I knew the deputy sheriff. He told me he would take me to the driver's license office. I had to pass the written exam. I knew how to drive already. In Japan, I drove my father's truck for his vegetable store. But in Japan, we drove on the left side, not the right. The deputy sheriff helped me out with the written exam; I had no problems.

Driving my first big car in the United States was awkward in the beginning. After about three hours driving, I was used to it. I could handle the car very well. I felt proud driving my first American car.

*****

I made the decision to go to Florida. I went to the wrestling office to see Leroy McGurik. I told him, "I would like to terminate my contract. I am going to Florida." I gave him enough notice, about one month until my finishing date. I planned to leave Oklahoma on December 15, and my start date in Florida was December 28 in Jacksonville. Leroy was disappointed that I was leaving, but he realized I had to move to other territories to grow as a wrestler.

My last day in the Oklahoma territory, I worked for Oklahoma TV. After I was finished, I called Duke Keomuka in Houston. I wanted to visit him before I moved to Florida. I drove from Oklahoma City to Dallas. From Dallas, I drove to Houston. I checked into a hotel in Houston. I called Duke. I believe it was December 17. I spent a few days in Houston visiting Duke and my other friends.

On Christmas day, Duke was going to a big celebration. He invited me to go with him. His friend, Pat Flanagan, was having a party. Pat owned a trailer business. He built trailers for the oil companies. Duke told me to meet him at Pat's house at nine o'clock in the morning. He said, "We have to start cooking the pig early."

There was a Hawaiian wrestler named Tyro Miyaki working in the Houston territory. He was a good friend of Duke's. When I arrived at Pat's house, Tyro Miyaki was already there. He was cooking the pig on a rotisserie with charcoal fire under it. The pig was turning very slowly. We had a few drinks while the pig was cooking. It took about eight hours to cook. When it was done, Tyro cut all the separate meat parts, and he made a beautiful display. He also cooked all Hawaiian food for the table like a buffet style. We had many different dishes to taste and to enjoy.

Many people had been invited to the party. All of Pat's friends and families, and all of Duke's friends and families. We were having a wonderful time, celebrating the holiday together.

After we ate dinner, we settled down to enjoy the rest of the evening. We were talking and listening to music. One woman asked me where I was going. She heard that I was only visiting Houston, and I was leaving the next day. I told her, "Tomorrow, I am driving to Florida." She looked at me very seriously and said, "I must warn you. You have to be careful when you go to Florida. You may get sand stuck in your shoes. There is beautiful white sand, and it gets in your shoes and never comes out!" I did not understand what she meant. I asked, "What do you mean sand gets stuck in your shoes?" She explained the whole story. She said people go to Florida, and they fall in love with it. They settle down there, and they never want to leave. Well, I did not believe her. I informed her that I had no intentions of settling down anywhere. I wanted to travel and to see the world. That was why I went into the wrestling business. Plus, I had seen, especially in the wrestling business, many guys get married and then divorced. I had seen too much. I had told myself that I would never get married, especially in my profession. I had to travel too much; I would never be home. I told all this to that woman.

She just laughed at me. She said, "Yes, I understand what you are saying, but still be very careful. That sand is beautiful and pure white."

11 FLORIDA

On December 26, 1962 I drove from Houston, Texas to Tampa, Florida, 1,100 miles. I drove about half of the distance to Pensacola, Florida. I rested there for the night. The next morning, I drove bound for Tampa. In those days, I drove on Highway 90 that goes from New Orleans to Tallahassee. Then, from Tallahassee, driving according to the map, I took Highway 27. Somewhere, I changed to Highway 41.

When I was around the Brooksville area, I saw a guy hitch-hiking. He was wearing a U.S. Navy uniform. He looked clean cut. Back then it was common to pick up a hitch-hiker. I was not suspicious or afraid. I stopped for him. He asked me where I was going. I told him I could drop him off in Tampa. He said that would be great. So, I had a companion for the rest of the trip to Tampa. When we arrived, he thanked me for the ride, and I drove to find a hotel.

I found a nice looking hotel. I checked in, found my room, and slept the rest of the night. The next morning, I went to the wrestling office at the Sportatorium. I introduced myself to Cowboy Luttrall, the promoter. He introduced me to Eddie Graham, the booker; to Skippy Jackson, Eddie's little brother and a referee; and to Bob Fleck, the book-keeper. The wrestling office welcomed me. Cowboy Luttrall said, "We are glad to have you in Florida, Hiro. Your first match is on December 28 in Jacksonville."

*****

The wrestling office told me they were expecting about 11,000 people at the Jacksonville show. It would be a sold out show.

Except for the house in St. Louis, this show would be the largest house I wrestled, yet.

On December 28, we left Tampa at two o'clock in the afternoon. I rode with Skippy Jackson, the referee. When we arrived at the Jacksonville Coliseum, there was a long line outside the building. I saw the program for the show in the dressing room. The Great Malenko and Eddie Graham were featured in the main event. It was a grudge match. I was in the fifth match. This was the first introduction of Hiro Matsuda in Florida.

My opponent that night was Reggie Parks from Phoenix, Arizona. I beat him. Then, I performed a karate demonstration in the middle of the ring. The fans were fascinated. My selling point was my Japanese martial arts.

*****

The cities in Florida were more modern than the cities in Oklahoma. They were more crowded, filled with different types of people. It was exciting for me, and it was a good change of pace. I grew up in a busy city. I enjoyed travelling to Jacksonville, Miami, and Tampa. Those cities had many people and many things to do.

In those days, on Friday night, we had a show in Miami Beach. After we finished in Jacksonville, we drove back to Tampa. The next day we went to Miami. We left at two o'clock in the afternoon. I had heard about Miami Beach, but this was the first time I saw it. The arena was called Miami Beach Auditorium. It held about 4,000 people. Next door, there was a large convention center, but we only used the auditorium. It was a convenient place for everyone. We always had about 3,500 to 4,000 people come to the show.

That night they introduced me in the ring. I noticed the fans looked different in Florida from the fans in Oklahoma. There was a completely different atmosphere.

After the match was over, we had to drive back to Tampa. We arrived at four o'clock in the morning. The next day, Saturday, we had a show in Lakeland, a city about 35 miles from Tampa. So, I worked half of a week for my first time in the Florida territory.

Sunday was the wrestlers day off. One of the wrestlers, the Great Malenko, lived near Clearwater Beach. His apartment was two blocks from the water tower, which is still there today. It was a great location close to the beach. Many of the boys lived on Clearwater Beach. I liked living in Tampa, though. Sometimes when we came home from a match, like Miami or Jacksonville, it was three or four o'clock in the morning when we arrived in Tampa. Then, if a wrestler lived in Clearwater, he had to drive another 45 minutes to get home. I did not want to go to Clearwater. However, on Sunday, it was very nice to visit Clearwater. I was invited to the Great Malenko's apartment. Many of the wrestlers visited. We had a barbeque outside, and we enjoyed the beach. We stayed all day having a great time.

I was surprised when I saw the beach at Clearwater. In Japan, the beach sand is dark brown. I had never seen white sand. Also, the sand was soft like a powder. I could not believe it. It was beautiful. When the woman in Houston warned me about the white sand getting stuck in my shoes, I did not understand. Now, I saw with my own eyes the incredible white sand.

*****

On Monday night, the show was in Orlando at the American Legion Hall. It held 2,000 people. Orlando was about 90 miles from Tampa. We drove on Highway 4, a four lane highway. The trip was easy; not much traffic back then. Orlando was a small city in those days. This was the first time I was introduced in Orlando.

On Tuesday night, I was introduced in Tampa at the Fort Homer H. Hesterly, the Armory. We wrestled in Sarasota on Wednesday night. The arena was small, only a capacity for 1,000 people. Sometimes, we were off on Wednesday. Then, we spent the day at the beach. On Thursday night, the show was in Jacksonville. After the match, usually we drove from Jacksonville all the way to Miami. This way we had a whole day to spend on Miami Beach before the show on Friday night.

We arrived in Miami around six o'clock in the morning. We checked into the hotel, paying for one day. The wrestlers liked to stay at The Hotel Promenade on Miami Beach. We slept until noon. Then, we went to the beach for the rest of the day. Miami Beach was very cosmopolitan; there were all kinds of people.

After the show that night, we drove back to Tampa. On Saturday night, we wrestled in Lakeland. Then, we rested on Sunday. That was the schedule I worked in the Florida territory.

*****

The Great Malenko was one of the top wrestlers. He wrestled as a Russian. His mother and his father were from Russia, but he was born in New Jersey. His trademark, though, was being a great Russian. In Miami, the Great Malenko took me to one of his favorite places to eat. He said, "Hiro, I will take you to eat food you have never tasted before now."

We went to a Jewish restaurant called Wolfie's. I did not know what Jewish food was. He told me they served corned beef. The only corned beef I knew was from a can in Japan. He asked me what I wanted to order. I had no idea what to order. This was his kind of food. I asked him to help me.

First, there was breakfast. I asked what to order. The Great Malenko told me to order a bagel with lox and cream cheese. When it came to me, I saw that the lox was smoked salmon. It tasted delicious. That became one of my favorite foods.

Then, when lunchtime came, after we had enjoyed the beach for a while, the Great Malenko said, "Let's go to Wolfies's again. For lunch you have to order a corned beef sandwich." I could not believe it; the sandwich was so big! The meat was about two inches thick. I had never seen a sandwich like this before. And the taste! It had a rich flavor. On the table, there were pickled cucumbers and coleslaw. We could eat as much as we wanted.

This was my first experience eating Jewish food. It was delicious. Whenever we were in Miami, we went to Wolfies's to eat.

*****

I became acquainted with the Florida towns and the wrestlers of the Florida territory. There were many top wrestlers, like the Great Malenko, Don Curtis, Eddie Graham, Yukon Eric, and The Kentuckian. I appreciated The Kentuckian's recommendation of me to the Florida office. I had the reputation for drawing a big house. The promoter wanted someone who could draw. However, now it was time to prove myself. It did not matter what great things other wrestlers said about me. The promoter wanted to see if I could draw or not.

For the first five weeks in the Florida territory, I was building my reputation. I was working hard to get people to know my name, Hiro Matsuda. One day in Miami Beach I was scheduled to wrestle Don Curtis. He was Eddie Graham's right hand man. He was an excellent wrestler, one of the top guys. This was a test for me. The promoter wanted to see what I could do.

Don Curtis had graduated from Buffalo University. He had been a great amateur wrestler. Then, he became a professional wrestler, and now he was working the best matches in Florida. At this time, my weight was 210 pounds. I had big, muscular legs and a rock hard, flat stomach. I had good size and a chip on my shoulder. We would have a good match against each other. The show was sold out.

The fifth match was when we would meet in the ring. We had a 20 minute time limit. The time started. We went against each other. We each wrestled with all our strength. I pinned him down, but he kicked out of it. Then, he had me down on the mat, and I got out of it. We kept going, back and forth. Neither man could get the best of the other. The time expired. It was a draw.

I had impressed everyone with my ability. We wrestled an intense 20 minute match, and Don Curtis could not beat me. I was equal with the top wrestlers. This match was my ticket to wrestling the main event.

*****

As time passed, I learned my way around the Florida territory. I had no problem finding my way anywhere. In Tampa, I was living in the south part of town in the Gandy Boulevard area. After the Tuesday night match, I did not want to hang-out with the other boys. I liked to have peace and quiet after I worked.

After the match, I sneaked out alone and went to my own place. There was a Chinese restaurant on the corner of Dale Mabry and Gandy. Sometimes I ate lunch there. Also, it had a nice bar. The MacDill Airforce Base was close by, so many pilots and officers used to go to the restaurant. The place was called Lama's. Also, the jai alai players went to the bar after their game. The players were well known, and they knew what it was like to not want to be bothered. Most of the guys from MacDill knew how to respect another person's privacy. Nobody bothered me at Lama's. I was able to enjoy my time alone.

Wherever I was after a match, I usually went to a bar alone. I did not need any company. I enjoyed going to the bar, sitting by myself for a couple of hours with no conversation, and having a few drinks. Every Tuesday in Tampa, I went to Lama's. The bartender got to know me. Then, he started to take care of me; he gave me free beer. But free beer was more expensive, because I tipped him even more money. I always had a nice night at the bar. It was quiet and relaxing for me.

The last call was at two-thirty in the morning. At the time, most restaurants were closed. The Waffle House was the only place open. I went there for breakfast. I ordered seven eggs, hash browns, and a double order of toast and sausage. I filled my stomach up. Then, I went back to my apartment to sleep. That was the end of the day.

*****

No matter what time I went to sleep at night, I woke up at nine-thirty in the morning. At ten o'clock I was in the gym. I spent a couple hours pushing weights and doing whatever I had to do that day to train. When I was finished training, I went back to my apartment. I cooked lunch at home. The simplest way to make a steak was to put it in the broiler. I made a pot of rice in the rice cooker. I also made a salad. That was my lunch every day. I ate a good steak, rice, and salad. The rest of the afternoon, I relaxed. Then, I went to wrestle that night.

*****

Before I moved to south Tampa, I stayed at a small hotel by the University of Tampa. The hotel was just before the bridge to downtown, on the right side going east to west, by the Hillsborough River. It is no longer there. A tall building replaced it. On Gasparilla Day, I could see the parade from my hotel room.

In those days, downtown Tampa was completely different. There were no big buildings. I still remember the Hillsborough Hotel. Also, there was the Bayview Hotel where the Barnett Building is now. The Thomas Jefferson Hotel was there. The old building of Maas Brothers and the Tampa Theater were downtown as well. It was popular to go downtown. There was a good night life back then. Many bars and restaurants were open. There were many places to go.

I will never forget. One night I went to a bar. The bartender asked me for my identification. I was 25 years old, but my Japanese face looked young. I was offended and angry that I had to show my identification. I did not understand. Now, I think it was funny. Anyway, downtown Tampa was a nice place to go. There was always somewhere to go, a place to find entertainment. I enjoyed living in Tampa.

*****

In those days, a few wrestlers worked the top. The Great Malenko was one. Also, a guy named Hans Mober from Holland was at the top. He worked wearing a mask like Zorro. Hans had a beautiful physique. One week later, after the match with Don Curtis, I became one of the top wrestlers in Florida territory.

The most popular wrestlers were Eddie Graham, Don Curtis, Yukon Eric, and The Kentuckian. Eddie Graham was the number one wrestler in Florida. He was the Southern Heavyweight Champion. I was working towards wrestling against him.

*****

I want to tell the story of Eddie Graham. He came from Chattanooga, Tennessee. The promoter, Cowboy Luttrall, was also from Chattanooga. When Cowboy Luttrall was wrestling, Eddie was a little boy. He used to carry the wrestling bags. Eddie started wrestling when he was 15 years old. Cowboy Luttrall took Eddie under his wing like he was his own son. Cowboy had a son who had been killed in the Korean War. Therefore, eventually when they came to Florida, Eddie and Cowboy became partners.

What I was told was this. When Cowboy was running the territory in 1957 and 1958, he only ran shows in the winter, because many tourists came to Florida. Wrestling was good business when the tourists were in Florida. But, in the summer, all the tourists went home. Cowboy closed the territory.

Before Eddie came to Florida to become partners with Cowboy, he wrestled in New York. He worked with his brother, Jerry. They were called the Graham Brothers. They used to pack the Madison Square Garden. Eddie made a name for himself. He used to draw people from all over the east coast. Wherever they wrestled, the show sold out.

Cowboy Luttrall asked Eddie one day, "Why don't you come down to Florida and make a home for yourself?" Eddie finished working in the New York territory. He moved to Florida. When Eddie came to Florida, he started opening the territory year round. The summer actually became bigger business than the winter. Eddie brought boys from New York to work in Florida. He built the territory up. Florida became the number one territory in the country.

The Florida office started working in relationship with Vince McMahon Sr. from the New York office. Boys from New York came to work in Florida, and boys from Florida went to New York to work. It was a great exchange. Both territories prospered.

*****

I was coming closer to wrestling in the main event. My reputation was getting bigger, ready to explode. Remember this was Tampa. It had been six weeks since I had come to Florida. Hiro Matsuda against the Southern Heavyweight Champion Eddie Graham, that was the future main event.

Finally, the day came for us to wrestle. The Fort Homer W. Hesterly, the Armory, was the place where we met in the ring. The show was sold out. Over 5,000 people came to see us wrestle. The people never expected that I would beat Eddie Graham. The match was great.

We wrestled for about 40 minutes. The people were thrilled. They gave us a standing ovation. The fans were angry, because I just beat their hero; however, they respected me. They were amazed at my wrestling ability. Now, I became the hero of Tampa. That was the first Southern Heavyweight Championship I won. My reputation was even stronger now.

*****

Wrestling was not everything. The wrestlers had goof-off, fun time too. Some of the wrestlers were very crazy. I was riding with Reggie Parks, coming back from Miami. He drove a 1962 Cadillac. We followed Highway 27 that had orange groves on both sides. Reggie pulled off the highway into an orange grove. I did not know why he did this at two o'clock in the morning. I said, "Reggie, what are you doing?" He laughed. He backed up into the orange grove, turned the lights off, opened the trunk, and started picking oranges.

I said, "Hey Reggie! What are you doing?" He said, "I am going to fill the trunk with oranges." I did not like this idea. If I was caught, I am in conspiracy with him. They would deport me back to Japan, because I was working under a visa. I was nervous. He was stealing oranges, but he was having fun. "I need oranges for the morning, " he said. He did not seem to realize he was stealing. Fortunately, we were safe, and we made it back to Tampa. When he dropped me off in Tampa, I was so happy and relieved. Reggie drove home to Clearwater.

Another incident happened when we had a spot show in Arcadia. It was about 80 miles from Tampa, south of Sarasota, in the middle of Florida. In the summer, watermelons grew in the fields on both sides of the highway. When I was riding with another crazy wrestler one time, he pulled over into the watermelon field. He picked a few watermelons and put them in the car. Then, we drove back to Tampa. I could not believe the jokes American boys played. They thought it was so funny.

*****

My reputation had grown to be the hottest in Florida. I corresponded with a newspaper reporter, Mr. Suzuki. We talked every week. He published my story in the pro wrestling magazine in Japan. I knew Rikidozan was aware of my success in the United States. I was becoming more popular than he was in the United States.

In Lakeland, there was a spring training camp for baseball. A Japanese team was participating with the Detroit Tigers. Mr. Suzuki had a friend who was a sportswriter reporting from the camp for

Nikon Sports. Mr. Suzuki asked him to see me in Tampa. We had dinner together.

He reported to Mr. Suzuki about my success. He told him I was the Southern Heavyweight Champion. This was proof that I was working the top in Florida. Mr. Suzuki wrote a big article about me for Nikon Sports and for the pro wrestling magazine.

Rikidozan and Mr. Suzuki were friends. Rikidozan told Mr. Suzuki, "I am very proud of Kojima."

*****

Two weeks later, I was notified that Lou Thesz was coming to Florida in a week. I was chosen to be his opponent. I was shocked and pleased. This match would be a dream come true. When I went to dinner with Duke Keomuka and Lou Thesz in Texas, I had told Lou Thesz that one day I would wrestle with him. He had told me he would look forward to it. Now, we were set to meet in the ring. I could hardly believe it! My heart beat rapidly with anticipation. This match would be the strongest proof I was at the top in the United States to all the wrestling fans in Japan.

The place was a packed house, about 5,600 people. Our match drew more people than ever. We set a record. The match was two out of three. I beat him in the first. Then, he beat me in the second. Unfortunately, I lost the last round. Lou Thesz won.

It was a great experience for me, though. Winning and losing meant nothing when I was wrestling an opponent like Lou Thesz. To me, he was like a god.

After the match, I met him in the dressing room. We shook hands. He told me, "Hiro, you wrestled skillfully. You did great. You have a bright future ahead of you. Keep it up. One day you will be known all over the United States."

*****

My trademark in wrestling was that I worked barefoot. When I went into the ring, I walked corner to corner on my tip toes showing off my beautiful, sexy legs. I had big, muscular legs, because every day I did 500 to 1,000 squats. All the girls said, "Oh! Hiro Matsuda has such sexy legs!"

One night, I was in the ring, walking corner to corner when I noticed a lady in a blue dress sitting ring-side. I looked at her and I thought, "What a gorgeous girl she is." The picture of her is in my memory forever. I remember passing by her showing off my sexy legs. But then, it was time for the match to begin. I had to forget about the girl, and I had to set my mind on wrestling that night.

About two weeks later, I found a note on my car. It was from the lady in the blue dress. Her name was Judy, and she asked me to meet her and a friend at a certain bar after the show. Plus, she left a phone number. After I read the note, I noticed there was another girl waiting for me in my car.

I asked her, "What are you doing in my car?" She told me, "My friends left me. You have to take me home. I live in Apollo Beach." I had no idea where Apollo Beach was. I wanted to go meet the lady in the blue dress, but I had to be a gentleman. I drove to Apollo Beach and back to Tampa. I did not know Apollo Beach was such a far drive. When I got to the bar, the lady in the blue dress was gone. It was one o'clock in the morning. It was too late.

The next day I called her. The phone number was for her work. I asked to speak with Miss Judy. When she came to the phone, I asked her for a date that night. It was Wednesday and I was off that night. Sometimes, on Wednesday I worked in Sarasota, but usually I was off. Miss Judy accepted my offer. She did not want me to pick her up at her house. We met at a bowling alley on south Dale Mabry. It was convenient, half way between where she lived and where I lived. Then, we went to the Hawaiian Village, a lounge that had a live band and a nice atmosphere. We had a few drinks and we danced together. We had a wonderful time. We talked and we enjoyed each other's company. When our date ended, we planned our next date.

*****

Eddie Graham and I became great opponents. Hiro Matsuda against Eddie Graham became the biggest drawing card in 1963. We wrestled in many different places. The people demanded to see us, especially in the major cities like Miami, Jacksonville, and Tampa. We worked together for about two months to hit all of Florida territory. We wrestled alone or as tag teams. It was the Great Malenko and I against Eddie Graham and Rick Steinbern, or The

Great Zorro and I against Eddie and Don Curtis. These combinations were popular in Florida. Later, Bob Alton, Sr. came to Florida. After he established himself, we also wrestled as partners.

One night, Eddie and I were scheduled to wrestle each other in the main event. We sold out every seat, 11,000 people. More people wanted to see us. There were about 5,000 people who were furious, because they could not get tickets for the show. That was how popular the match, Eddie Graham against Hiro Matsuda, was.

*****

A good friend of mine, Tito Kopa, wanted to come to Florida territory to wrestle. He had gone back to Argentina for a few months, and now he wanted to return to the United States to wrestle. I spoke with Cowboy Luttrall. I made arrangements for Tito Kopa to come into Florida from Buenos Aires.

He spent about four months in Florida. We had a great time. He was a hell of a cook, and he knew how to have fun. Tito was a small size wrestler. He turned out to be a mediocre card. He did not stay long.

However, when he was here, every Sunday we had a great time. A few wrestlers got together on the Causeway. We took the barbecue with us. We spent all day on the beach. Tito barbecued for us Argentinian style. He made chimichurri sauce. We drank a few beers, ate chimichurri barbeque, and enjoyed the beach. When people came by us, they recognized us wrestlers. They saw all of us relaxing, having a great time.

*****

In the middle of the year 1963, we started wrestling another program. A promoter from Puerto Rico had heard about the strong wrestling business in Florida. Eddie Graham and I were invited to San Juan, Puerto Rico.

The first time in Puerto Rico, the promoter gave us rooms at the best hotel on San Fran beach. We flew in that morning, checked into our hotel, and wrestled that night. It was a Saturday night show. We wrestled at the baseball stadium. On Sunday morning, we flew back to Florida. We did a great business, and the promoter wanted us to come back. For about four weeks, I went to Puerto Rico for the Saturday night show. I wrestled against Eddie or the local wrestlers.

During those four weeks, I became well-known in Puerto Rico. I spoke Spanish so I felt very comfortable. It reminded me of Mexico. I enjoyed the change. I had a wonderful time in Puerto Rico.

*****

Another place we went to wrestle was the Bahamas. We wrestled in Nassau and Freeport once a month. We flew in early and spent the whole day at the beach. It was beautiful. The water was the color of emeralds. We wrestled that night. Then, the following morning, we flew back to Tampa.

Sometimes we rented snorkels during the day. We swam in the emerald water, looking at the exotic fish. We soaked up sun on the beach. We ate good food like conch salad, conch chowder, fried grouper, and fried bananas. We drank a tropical drink, rum with pineapple juice. We really enjoyed it. We were taking a break from the Florida territory, having fun, and earning extra money.

*****

We used to wrestle on Monday in Orlando, and in another town called Lake Worth near West Palm Beach. Some of the boys went to Orlando; some went to Lake Worth.

On Tuesday night, most of the top wrestlers worked in Tampa at Fort Homer W. Hesterly, the Armory. The second place wrestlers went to work was Fort Myers.

On Wednesday, we worked a small town near Sarasota. Sometimes, we were off for the day.

We drove 200 miles from Tampa on Thursday. We followed Highway 41 to Highway 301 to Jacksonville. Highway 75 did not exist back then. The scenery was great along 41 and 301. There were many orange groves, and we stopped along the way to drink fresh orange juice. It was not a bad drive.

Florida wrestling season was busy from January to the end of August. Business slowed down when school started. September and October were very slow. Then, around Thanksgiving, the business picked up. There was always a huge show around the holidays in December.

12 TRAINING WITH KARL GOTCH

During 1963 I heard about Karl Gotch, a famous wrestler from Europe. He had an over- abundance of wrestling knowledge. His reputation was great all over the world. One night I had dinner with Don Curtis at Don's house. He told me he knew Karl Gotch quite well. I asked Don, "Please, introduce me to Karl Gotch. I have been hearing his name for so long. I want to spend time with him to learn all that he knows about wrestling."

Don called Karl Gotch. At that time, Karl was living about 20 miles outside of Columbus, Ohio. Don introduced me over the phone. I told Karl I had heard of his reputation, and I would like the opportunity to train with him. He told me I was welcome to come see him. It was the end of October when I met Karl by telephone.

I told Cowboy Luttrall that I wanted to take two to three months off. I planned to go see Karl Gotch to learn more about wrestling. One of the main reasons I wanted to learn from Karl Gotch was because I had my mind set on wrestling Rikidozan one day. I would learn wrestling techniques from Karl Gotch to prepare myself to meet Rikidozan when I return to Japan.

I drove from Tampa to Columbus, 1,100 miles. I had to go through Highway 301, pass Charlotte, North Carolina. Then, I took Highway 21 all the way up to the mountains, and back down to Ohio. Finally, I arrived at Karl Gotch's house. He was waiting for me.

There was an old promoter, Al Haft. He was a millioniare. He had invested money in real estate. He owned most of the land around where Karl lived. He also had a hotel. Al Haft told me I could stay in his hotel at a discounted rate. Al owned a barn that had a wrestling ring upstairs. It was convenient for Karl Gotch and me to train.

Karl said to me, "If you can keep up with me, you could be in great shape." I was 25 years old; he was 37 years old. Karl was in excellent shape. Every morning after breakfast, I met Karl at his house. We went back into the woods. He lived in a subdivision, but behind his house, there was a nice park and woods. In the woods, we could climb up and down the ground as we ran. We ran single first. Then, he carried me on his shoulders as he ran, and after his turn, I carried him on my shoulders as I ran. We would go up and down the hills. Next, he grabbed my feet, and I walked on my hands, like I was a wheelbarrow. Then, I grabbed his feet and steered him on his hands. We spent 45 minutes to one hour doing those exercises. In the middle of nowhere, we stopped and did push-ups. After 40 to 50 push-ups, we got up and started running again. We worked out for one hour and 30 minutes without stopping.

Next, we went to Al Haft's barn, upstairs to the ring. We started to wrestle. He showed me different moves. I tried to pick up everything I could. I only had three months to learn.

Sometimes, it snowed outside, but we dressed in warm sweat suits. We ran the same routine in the snow, in the rain, in the sun. It did not matter. We never missed a day. Only on Sunday, we rested. We trained six days a week.

In the evening, he invited me to his house to eat dinner. Ella, his wife, was from Belgium. She was a superb cook. She made food from Germany, Belgium, and Holland. I tasted food I had never had before. She made sausage, potato pancakes, and many other kinds of food. I had a wonderful time eating her food. Everything she cooked was delicious.

When I was training with Karl Gotch, I received a letter from a girl in Japan. She went to the same grammar school as I did. I met her when I was waiting for a train at Tsurumi Station, my neighborhood station. It was just before I left Japan. I had all my papers ready, and I was waiting for my departure date. I was at the train station, waiting for my train to Tokyo, when we saw each other. I had not seen her since grammar school. She was in college now. She said, "Kojimasan! I still remember you!" I said, "I remember you, too!" She asked me what I was doing. I told her I was preparing to leave the country to go to South America. I planned to wrestle professionally and travel all over the world. She was happy to see me. She asked me if I ever have a chance, would I please write her a letter. We corresponded once in a while.

Therefore, when I was training with Karl Gotch, I received a letter from this girl. The letter said, "Rikidozan was stabbed with a knife in a night club." There was a newspaper article enclosed. The wound was not serious, and he would be released from the hospital in two weeks. Then, her next letter said, "Rikidozan had died. He got an infection in the wound, and he died." When I read that letter my heart dropped, because I had so much ambition to see Rikidozan. I wanted to prove to him that he was wrong, and that I had been right. I did not have to make my name as a sumo wrestler or judo master or whatever in order to be a successful professional wrestler. I had made it on my own. Also, I was training with the best wrestler in the world, Karl Gotch.

I wanted the opportunity to say to Rikidozan, "If you want to try to wrestle with me, you can try anytime, anyplace. I will prove my skill to you. I will beat you anytime, anyplace you want." But, now that opportunity was lost. I lost my heart. I lost my focus. Now, my only goal was to earn money.

spent time with Karl Gotch through Christmas. At Christmas time, all of his German friends got together to celebrate. We had a joyous holiday. Then, after Christmas, it was time to go. I told Karl, "Thank you very much. What you have done for me, I will never forget." I also thanked Ella for the delicious food. I drove back to Florida.

13 BACK IN FLORIDA
MISS JUDY
OKLAHOMA

When I returned to Florida, I put even more effort into professional wrestling. I went back to the same wrestling routine. Plus, I saw Miss Judy, the lady in the blue dress. We started dating regularly. We spent many of our dates walking on Clearwater Beach at night, or we spent the day at the beach, or we went to the Hawaiian Village to have a drink, to listen to music, and to dance. We had a great time together.

The time passed quickly. Soon, it was summer. Just before school summer break, Leroy McGuirk called Cowboy Luttrall. Leroy wanted to send Danny Hodge to Florida. Cowboy Luttrall told him he had a great opponent for Danny. Hiro Matsuda against Danny Hodge in Florida would be a sold out show.

Leroy McGuirk and Danny Hodge left Oklahoma and came to Florida. After about three weeks, Danny Hodge established himself. Then, we met in Tampa at Fort Homer W. Hesterly, the Armory. It was the World Junior Heavyweight Championship match.

I knew I would beat him this time. I had confidence. This was a great opportunity. We wrestled in the best two out of three rounds for the match. I beat him. The people were shocked. The wrestling fans did not expect that Hiro Matsuda would beat Danny Hodge for the World Junior Heavyweight Championship.

Leroy McGuirk took a video tape of the match to Oklahoma. He showed all of Oklahoma territory. The people saw Hiro Matsuda beat Danny Hodge. They went crazy. Leroy McGuirk wanted me to come to Oklahoma to work again. He made the arrangements with

Cowboy Luttrall. Danny Hodge stayed in Florida and I went back to Oklahoma.

I told Miss Judy I was going to Oklahoma. I invited her. I said, "If you can get off work, I would like you to accompany me to Oklahoma. I will show you the territory." She made arrangements to get off work, and we left for Oklahoma together. We had a wonderful time traveling from Tampa, through Tallahassee. When we passed Tallahassee, the water pump in my car broke. We were in Fort Walton, Florida. We had to stay over one night, because a new water pump had to be put in my car. Then, we stopped in New Orleans. I showed her my favorite places in New Orleans. We went up Highway 65 to Mississippi. She had never seen these southern states. We drove by cotton fields. We stopped at little restaurants on the highway. We enjoyed the time driving, keeping each other company.

In those days a 1959 Dodge did not have air conditioning. Four windows rolled down all the way, that was our air conditioning. We did not mind. It was very hot, but we were having a great time driving together. Finally, we reached Little Rock, Arkansas, our first destination of the Oklahoma wrestling territory.

*****

When Miss Judy and I drove into Little Rock, we found a nice hotel. I wrestled that night, and Miss Judy waited for me at the hotel. After the show, I picked her up. We went to a restaurant to have dinner. We had a great time talking and eating good food.

The wrestling fans in Little Rock knew I had beat Danny Hodge in Florida. When I stepped into the ring, I was even more popular than I was in 1962. People were angry that I had beat Danny. Now, I was more mature. My body was heavier. When I was wrestling in 1962, I weighed 208 pounds; now, I weighed 230 pounds. The wrestling fans screamed at me, "You Jap! You wait until Danny Hodge comes back! He is going to beat your ass!" I yelled back at them, "Beat my ass, you say? Just wait and see who gets a beating!"

We stayed in Little Rock for one week. I showed Miss Judy all around Little Rock. Then, we headed for Springfield, Missouri. We left Little Rock early in the morning. We took our time driving. We drove through the mountains, and we stopped at many places along the way. When we arrived in Springfield, we checked into a hotel. We planned to stay in Springfield for one week. I wrestled a show in Springfield. Then, Miss Judy and I spent the rest of the time vacationing like tourists.

After Springfield, we drove to Tulsa, Oklahoma. One of the boys told me about a great steak house called Jamel's. He said that I should take my girlfriend to dinner there. An old house had been converted into the restaurant. We both ordered steaks. The flavor was extraordinary. Miss Judy said she had never tasted steak like that. We both enjoyed that night very much.

We also found a nice Chinese restaurant. We liked to try different places to eat. We always had a good time, eating good food, having a few drinks, and talking to each other.

Our vacation together came to an end. Miss Judy had to return to Tampa, Florida. I stayed in Oklahoma another three months. I toured the territory, wrestling in the same cities I had in 1962. I enjoyed seeing those places again. It was a good change from Florida.

*****

After I had been working in the Oklahoma territory for three weeks, Danny Hodge returned. We wrestled the same shows, but we had different opponents. We did not wrestle each other, yet. People saw me wrestle. They saw Danny wrestle. They wanted to see us wrestle against each other.

I was defending his old title, the Junior Heavyweight Championship. He was working underneath me, wrestling other opponents. The people were getting so mad. For about two weeks, people watched me defend the championship, and Danny did not get a championship match, yet.

After four weeks, finally I met Danny Hodge in the World Junior Heavyweight Championship match. We wrestled all over the Oklahoma territory in different cities. Every place we went, the show was sold out. It was the first time that every city had a sold out show. The promoter, Leroy McGuirk, never expected it.

Our match was demanded to be seen by all the wrestling fans. One night we went 60 minutes. Then, another night, we wrestled for 60 minutes again. We wrestled to the end of the time limit and neither of us won. It was a draw. Finally, we wrestled for a 90 minute match. By the end of 90 minutes, I could not sweat anymore. I was completely dehydrated. Danny was in the same condition. But, I successfully defended my title.

I wanted to have different opponents. I did not want to keep wrestling Danny Hodge only. I knew I could draw if I had a good American opponent. However, the promoter was banking everything on Danny Hodge and Hiro Matsuda matches. That was a mistake. I knew when Danny and I were finished wrestling each other, I was not going to make any money. After three months, I spoke with Leroy McGuirk. I asked him what his plans were for different opponents for me. He had not prepared any opponents for me. I told him that it was time for me to go home. Four years had passed since I left Japan. I was ready to go back. I gave Leroy my notice, and I told him that in the future I would like to return to Oklahoma.

I finished my work in the Oklahoma territory. My last night, I wrestled Danny in Oklahoma City. Danny Hodge beat me. I did not care. I was tired of our rivalry. After that, I went back to Florida.

14 THE RETURN HOME
JAPAN

When I came back to Florida, it was the end of October. I was preparing to go back to Japan. Just before I left for Japan, I was wrestling in a match one night, and I sprained my bad ankle, the one I broke in Fort Worth, Texas in 1961. I could not walk on my ankle; I had crutches. I got on the airplane with crutches.

The time came to leave Tampa. Miss Judy and I went to the airport together. We said good-bye, and I got on the plane. I could see Miss Judy from the airplane window. She waited there until the plane left the gate. I knew I was coming back to Florida, but the future is uncertain. I was very sad leaving her in Florida. I had a beautiful eight by ten photograph of Miss Judy to take with me to Japan.

When the plane arrived in Tokyo, I saw about 500 people waiting to welcome me. After four years and seven months of successful wrestling overseas, Hiro Matsuda returned to Japan. It struck me as funny to have that many people waiting for me. I also felt proud and happy. Now, I had many fans who were excited to see me. I had achieved my dream of becoming a successful professional wrestler in the United States. I was an inspiration to many people.

I did not want to use my crutches when I got off the airplane. I walked, not limping, so no one could see I had a sprained ankle. I went through immigration and customs. Once I got out of customs, there were many wrestling fans cheering for me and welcoming me home. My father's friends and their sons made a "Hiro Matsuda Support Club". They were holding a banner that said, "Hiro Matsuda! Welcome to Japan!" There were many reporters from different newspapers. Everyone treated me like a hero. I had never experienced anything like this. It was overwhelming and exciting. I felt great. To myself, I was wishing that Rikidozan was alive. I wished he could see me. That is what I was missing the most in that moment.

*****

From the airport, we went to my family home. My mother, my father, and my sister were happy I was home with them. My parents and neighbors made a big celebration party for me. We ate sushi and drank beer and sake. Everyone in the neighborhood came to our house to welcome me home. My parents were proud. After four years and seven months, I had returned home. My mother cried every night I had been gone, missing her son. She was happy and relieved to see me finally. She was so proud that I was successful overseas, and I had become famous.

When I left Japan in 1960, I told my parents, "I have a one way ticket. If I never make a success of my dream, I will never step on Japanese soil again." My parents understood the nature of my feelings. If I said that, then I would do it; therefore, they prayed I would make a success overseas and then return one day. Inside my heart I knew that once I had the opportunity, I would make it all the way to the top of the wrestling business. I had confidence. No one else knew that. Only Hiro Matsuda knew this.

*****

After Rikidozan died, Toyonobori took over as president of Japan Pro Wrestling. Yoshino Sato was the vice president. Toyonobori and Yoshino Sato, along with Yoshihara, trained me when I first started wrestling in Japan. Japan Pro Wrestling welcomed me home. They introduced me on the Friday night television show. The ratings for that show went so high that Japan Pro Wrestling wanted me to stay in Japan to wrestle. However, I had another plan. I had a commitment to go back to Florida. Miss Judy was waiting for me, and I wanted to live in the United States of America.

I stayed in Japan for one and a half months. During my time, I was commentating at the matches. I went to many press meetings. I was getting so much publicity all over Japan. It felt wonderful. I was having a great time. The people expected me to stay in Japan. But after one and a half months, it was time to return to the United States.

15 BACK IN AMERICA
MARRIAGE
A NEW LIFE

When I was at home in Japan, I had the eight by ten photograph of Miss Judy in my room. It was a beautiful photo in a nice frame. My mother and my father saw the picture. They did not ask me about her. They did not need an explanation. They knew if I had a photograph of a beautiful American girl, then I felt seriously about her.

When I returned to Tampa, Florida, I was happy to see Miss Judy again, and she was happy to see me. We continued dating regularly. Then, one night we had a huge argument. I was very hot headed and short tempered in my young years. We broke up.

I had an opportunity to go to Amarillo, Texas to wrestle. Dory Funk, Sr. was the promoter. He and Eddie Graham were good friends. Florida territory and Amarillo used to exchange boys. Dory needed me. Plus, my good friend Don Curtis and his wife, Dotty, were wrestling in Amarillo. The timing was just right. I did not want to see Miss Judy anymore, so I left. I told myself that I would never come back to Florida.

I did not realize how much I would miss her. I thought I would leave Miss Judy and forget her. The funny thing was that I really missed her. But, I was bull-headed and too proud. Every day I fought myself. I said to myself, "You are Hiro Matsuda! You are a man! You are a Japanese man! Forget about her!" Then, my heart would tell me, "You better call her! You do not want to lose Miss Judy!" My mind would say, "No! Be a strong man!" Finally, my heart won the fight.

Don and Dotty Curtis were very good friends to me. I spoke to them about Miss Judy. They encouraged me to call her. I gave in, and I called Miss Judy. The most important call I ever made.

When I finished my commitment in Amarillo, I returned to Tampa. I went to Miss Judy, my lady in the blue dress. I proposed marriage. Fortunately, she accepted. Our wedding was on June 19, 1965.

*****

We went on our honeymoon to Puerto Rico and the Virgin Islands. In 1962, I had wrestled in Puerto Rico, and I wanted to take Judy to show her how beautiful and historical it was. Also, I had heard that St. Thomas of the Virgin Islands was a romantic place with beautiful water. That was why we chose those two islands for our honeymoon.

Duke Keomuka had a friend from Dallas who owned a hotel in San Fran, Puerto Rico. Duke made arrangements with his friends for us to stay at his hotel. It was called La Concha Hotel, a first class hotel on the beach. We checked into the hotel. When we entered our room, there was a big, gorgeous basket of fruit on the table. It said, "Welcome!" on it. A little while later, there was a knock on the door. The owner of the hotel stopped by our room to greet us and to make sure we were comfortable. He had just flown in from Dallas. That was very nice of him to welcome us. We felt quite comfortable, like we were at home.

During the day, we enjoyed the beach. We drank pina coladas. We swam in the beautiful water. We toured the island seeing many historical sights. At night, we went out to eat at native restaurants. The food was delicious. Judy tasted food she never had before then. We had a wonderful time in Puerto Rico. We stayed for three days. Then, we went to the Virgin Islands.

When we reached the Virgin Islands, we checked into our hotel. We rested for the night. After a good sleep, we woke early the next morning. A bus came to the hotel to pick us up and take us to Sapphire Beach. The water was turquoise and crystal clear. We snorkeled and saw many different tropical fish. At night, we enjoyed the entertainment at the hotel. We ate a nice dinner. Then, a singer performed. Later, we listened to island music. We had a few tropical drinks, and we danced. We had a romantic time.

Our honeymoon vacation came to an end. We returned to Tampa, Florida. Now, it was time to start building our life together.

16 TENNESSEE

I began wrestling in Florida again. It was summer, 1965. The Tennessee territory was hurting in business, because their shows were not drawing many people. They did not have good wrestlers. The promoters asked Eddie and Cowboy Luttrall for help. However, the Tennessee promoter had a reputation for treating wrestlers unfairly. Even if the boys drew good money, the pay-off was low. The boys did not want to go to Tennessee to work. They were desperate for help.

Because Florida and Tennessee had a business relationship, Eddie Graham and Sam Steamboat decided to go to wrestle in Tennessee once a week. I agreed to go to help. At that time Antonio Inoki was wrestling in Dallas. Duke was working in Florida and Texas. They both decided to go to Tennessee to help, too. We got together in Tennessee. Every week we put on great shows. We were beating so many guys our reputations grew strong. Eddie Graham and Sam Steamboat were the World Tag Team Champions. Inoki and I went against them. The wrestling fans liked to see us go against their champions.

Judy and I had a great time together in Tennessee. A friend of mine knew the owner of a trailer park in Nashville. He introduced us. Judy and I rented a house trailer for our new home. It was a nice place to live.

Inoki and I became established in Tennessee. We wrestled for the Memphis television in a match against Eddie Graham and Sam Steamboat. We wrestled two out of three. Inoki and I won two straight. We were the new World Tag Team Champions. People were stunned. The tape went all over Tennessee. After the tape was seen, the people were anxious to see us in live shows.

The first night we were defending the Championship against Eddie Graham and Sam Steamboat was in Memphis. It was snowing badly. I thought no one would show up. When we arrived at the arena that evening, there was a long line around the building. I could not believe it. How did people get there through that heavy snow, I wondered. Inoki and I went into the dressing room. Eddie and Sam were flying from Tampa to Memphis, but they got stuck in Birmingham, Alabama. The plane had to land there, because the weather was so bad. The show was sold out. We did not have an opponent. The promoter quickly came up with another opponent. The people wanted to see us wrestle Eddie Graham and Sam Steamboat, but they would have to wait. We wrestled a great match, and the fans were satisfied.

I expected a big pay-off, because the show had been sold out. There were about 7,000 people at the show. We brought in a lot of money. When I received my pay, it was only $100. I told the promoter, "You must be making a mistake." He said, "No, there is no mistake. That is the amount you earned." I replied, "If you are not making a mistake, then you are not going to see me anymore."

I called the office in Florida. I explained the situation. I wanted to help the Tennessee territory, but the promoter was not living up to his promise. I could not accept $100 for what was supposed to be an $800 pay-off. I told the office I planned to give my notice. They understood. That ended our business relationship. Eddie and Sam quit the territory, also. Inoki went to Hawaii and then to Japan. Judy and I went back to Florida.

17 1965 – 1967
FLORIDA
WORLD TOUR
JAPAN

In 1965, the Florida office offered a percentage of ownership to a few of the top wrestlers in Florida. The office wanted to keep us in Florida, so they offered each of us a percentage of the company. Duke and I talked about it. We thought it would be a good investment. Therefore, I stayed in Florida longer than I expected. My original idea was to travel to different territories. I could spend one year in the Carolinas, one year in Texas, one year in New York, and where ever else I chose to go. Once I bought into the business though, I became interested in promoting shows and making money. I was receiving revenue every month from the share I bought in the business. Many promoters from different territories wanted me to wrestle for them, but my first priority was taking care of my own business in Florida. Therefore, I settled in Tampa, Florida.

*****

Yoshino Sato called me in 1966. He was now President of Japan Pro Wrestling. He asked me to return to Japan to wrestle. Since my visit in 1964, people had been waiting to see me wrestle. The fans saw me introduced in the ring, and they saw the publicity for me. They were anxious to see me wrestle at live shows.

I asked Duke if he wanted to go to Japan. He was delighted. We traveled to Japan together. Sometimes, we wrestled as a team; other times we wrestled singles. All the people were waiting to see me. I was the new star of Japan. At every place I wrestled, the show was sold out. The people wanted to see Hiro Matsuda.

We traveled through Japan for one month. This was Duke's first time in Japan. He was having a wonderful time. The wrestling was good, but the sight-seeing was the most exciting part for him. It felt great to me to be so popular. I had truly achieved my dream. This was the first time and the last time I wrestled in Japan on a big scale. This was the only time I wrestled for Japan Pro Wrestling.

Yoshihara had retired from wrestling. He was working for the Japan Pro Wrestling office. While I was touring in Japan, he talked to me about a grievance he had with the company. He did not agree with the way the office conducted the business. Yoshihara wanted to quit Japan Pro Wrestling. He planned to create his own company and run the opposition. Yoshihara asked me to join him.

I was a good friend to Yoshihara. He had trained me when I first started wrestling. We had a long history together. I felt compassionate toward him and his situation. I agreed to help him.

*****

After the 1966 Japan tour finished, Judy joined me in Tokyo. We planned to travel on an around the world trip. First, we spent a few days in Yokohama visiting my family. Then, I showed her parts of Japan.

From Tokyo, we flew Japan Airlines to Europe. We flew from Tokyo to Bangkok to Tehran and to our first destination, Cairo. At the airport in Cairo we went through customs and immigration. Judy had no problem, because she had an American passport. Immigration took a longer time to clear me. Finally, we took a taxi to our hotel in downtown Cairo. As we drove, we saw many people sleeping on the side of the streets. Neither of us had ever seen anything like that. When we arrived at our hotel, the man at the counter said we were too early to check-in. Our room was not ready. We had just traveled over 24 hours. I argued with the man to let us check-in to our room. He refused us.

An old porter overheard what was happening with us. He was furious. He told the man at the counter, "These people have traveled so far for such a long time; we need to show them some courtesy." We left our luggage with the desk, and the porter took us to a restaurant to eat. He drove us around the city for a little while, and then took us back to our hotel. Finally, our room was ready. Our room was on a high floor with a view of the Nile River. That night we rested to recover from our long journey.

We went on a tour of the Pyramids the next day. We rode camels through the Pyramids. We saw the Sphynx. We spent the whole day touring the historical places. After our tour, we returned to the hotel. We ate a delicious dinner at the hotel restaurant. We stayed in Cairo for two days.

Next, we flew to Athens, Greece. We stayed there for a couple of days, also. We toured the ancient Greek historical places. We went downtown and ate dinner at a wonderful Greek restaurant.

After Athens, we flew to Rome, Italy. We did not have a hotel reservation. We found a cozy, small hotel. We went to see the Vatican, the Coliseum, and other historical sights. We enjoyed the atmosphere of Rome.

From Rome we went to Zurich, Switzerland. We arrived in Zurich without a hotel reservation. At the airport, we asked where we should go. They told us to stay at City Hotel. It was a small, but wonderful place. When we checked into the hotel, they told us a tour was leaving in thirty minutes. We put our luggage in our room, and we rushed to meet with the tour group. We went all around Zurich. They took us to a special place to eat cheesecake. We expected the cheesecake like we had in America, but it was not sweet. It did have a delicious flavor. After the tour, we went back to the hotel. We walked to a nearby lake. There was an outside orchestra performing. We sat down and listened to the music. Many people were enjoying the nice night. We drank wine and ate some food. We were having a splendid time.

From Zurich we flew to Madrid, Spain. I had a wrestler friend, Mariano, who lived in Madrid. I had met him when he was working in the United States. He met us at the airport, and he took us downtown to the Plaza Hotel. We had arrived early in the day. We settled into our hotel. Then, we went to a bullfight at night. After the bullfight, we went back into town. It was twelve-thirty in the morning and the streets were packed with people. During the day, the people take a two hour siesta. Then, they stay up late at night into the early morning hours. People eat dinner at ten or eleven o'clock at night. I was comfortable speaking Spanish, so Judy and I wandered the city alone. We went to cafes and bars, getting a taste of the night life of Madrid. The next night, Mariano took us to an outside restaurant. The special dish was the roast lamb. We ate delicious Spanish food and drank many bottles of wine.

After Madrid, we flew to Paris. We checked into our hotel near the Eiffel Tower. We spent a couple of days in Paris. We toured the city, looking at all the French historical sights.

From Paris, we took the train to Antwerp, Belgium. We had to change trains in Brussels. We were carrying two suitcases and rushing to catch our train. We almost missed the train to Antwerp. Finally, we reached Antwerp, Belgium. Karl Gotch's daughter, Genean, was living there with her grandmother. They were waiting for us to arrive. They took us to a small hotel by the train station. We went to their house for dinner. The grandmother cooked a delicious dinner for us. We had a great time visiting with them.

In Antwerp the food was outstanding. The pastries were wonderful. Also, as we walked the streets, we bought fried potatoes with vinegar and mustard, a tasty snack. Near the hotel we went to a restaurant. We saw a pig roasting in the window. We ordered the roasted pork, and we had a drink called a Trappist, dark beer with grenadine in it. It was very good. Judy loved it.

Antwerp was an old port city with a great history. Karl Gotch's mother was 75 years old. She took us all over the city on a walking tour, and she told us the history of her home. We went to a beautiful zoo. It was one of the best zoos in Europe we were told. We spent a whole day there. It was amazing.

We were in Antwerp for three days. We had a wonderful time. We thanked Genean and her grandmother, and we said good-bye. Then, we took the train to the end of the continent. From there, we rode a boat across the English Channel to Dover, England. From Dover, we took the train to London.

When we arrived in London, we did not have a hotel reservation. Judy called places from the train station. We found a neat, small hotel. We enjoyed touring London and seeing all the different places in the city. When we went to a bar, we asked for a cold beer. They did not serve cold beer, only room temperature beer. After walking around outside all day, we wanted a nice cold beer, but we had to drink warm beer. It was a different experience. We found a good Chinese restaurant for dinner. London had many different cultures. We stayed in London for a couple of days.

From London we were going to go to New York, but there was an airline strike in the United States. We had to fly to Nassau, Bahamas. We did not plan to go to the Bahamas. It was a pleasant detour. We stayed on Emerald Beach for one day. Then, we flew home to Tampa, Florida.

*****

After we returned to Florida, I was preparing for the new corporation in Japan with Yoshihara in 1967. Yoshihara was working with wrestlers in Japan, and I was preparing the right kind of American wrestler to go to Japan. Our first priority was to prove to the television station that we could run a successful show. Without the television station, there was no way we could have a successful business. Yoshihara had a friend at the Tokyo Broadcasting Station. He was the program director, and he was interested in our business. He did not make any promises. We had to show him what we could do.

Before we started our business, another group started a corporation called Tokyo Pro Wrestling. Inoki, Toyonobori, and Shimma ran the business. They only lasted three months. They went bankrupt. At the time when Yoshihara and I started our company, Inoki was available. I asked him if he wanted to work with us. He agreed.

For the first show, I sent Bill Dromo, Roger Coby, and Stacy Hall. We ran the show to prove our capabilities to Tokyo Broadcasting Station. We did not draw many people, but the station saw our potential. We put together an exciting show.

For our second tour, I took The Kentuckian, Eddie Graham, and Sam Steamboat to Japan with me. The television station was impressed with these big American boys. We had a show in a city in Kyushu. Tokyo Broadcasting Station had an affiliate station there. They wanted to see what kind of ratings we could achieve. The place was packed. We had good promotions. We had close to 70% ratings. Tokyo Broadcasting Station decided to do business with us.

Yoshihara and I were happy. We were going to beat Japan Pro Wrestling. Tokyo Broadcasting Station was bigger than Nippon

Television Station. Nippon was the station that Japan Pro Wrestling used. We were excited about our future success.

I went back to the United States to prepare for our next tour. In the meantime, Yoshihara brought another partner into the business without consulting me. I did not understand why he did this. Yoshihara and I agreed to be 50% - 50% partners. Yoshihara would find the financial investors, and I would supply all the talent. That was our deal. Now, our arrangement would have to change with another partner. I pulled out of the business. Yoshihara and the new partner flew to Florida to persuade me to stay with them, but I adamantly refused. I gave them my resignation.

Yoshihara ran the business without me. It lasted for three years. The business folded, because they did not have enough American wrestlers. I believe the business had a great potential, because I had many contacts in the United States. Plus, the Japanese wrestling fans were eager to see me again. They had watched me wrestle in 1966, and now they wanted Hiro Matsuda to return. Also, I could have trained other Japanese boys to be great wrestlers.

During my time in Japan working with Yoshihara, before I resigned, Judy gave birth to our first daughter, Heather. It was unfortunate that I could not be there when she was born. I was creating the future business in Japan. We were even planning to move there. However, since the arrangement between Yoshihara and I did not work out, I decided not to return to Japan.

At the end of 1967, Jim Crockett, Sr., the promoter of Charlotte, North Carolina called Cowboy Luttrall. They were good friends. Jim Crockett wanted me to wrestle for the North Carolina territory. Cowboy Luttrall came to me. He said, "Hiro, you are going to North Carolina in December."

18 NORTH CAROLINA

In early December 1967, I went to Charlotte, North Carolina alone to get settled in the area before moving my family there. When I arrived in Charlotte for the first time, I stayed at the Roving Court Motel where all the wrestlers stayed. It was convenient, because I could ride with other wrestlers to the shows. One of the wrestlers, Larry Hamilton, told me about the Green Oak Apartments where he lived. He said it was a nice place with a good manager. There was a two bedroom apartment available. I made arrangements with the manager to rent the apartment. Then, I went back to Tampa, Florida to get my family.

We stayed in Tampa through Christmas. After the holidays, Judy and I packed up our belongings. At this time, my sister, Hatsue, was visiting us. She stayed with us for six months. Hatsue, Judy, Heather, and I drove together all the way to Charlotte. We had a two car convoy. Judy drove one car; I drove the other. We arrived in Charlotte safely. We moved into our new home at the Green Oak Apartments.

I had spent three weeks in Charlotte establishing my wrestling name before bringing my family. After wrestling two more weeks, my reputation was strong enough that I could wrestle singles. However, Charlotte was a tag team territory. Jim Crockett, Sr. set me up with Larry Hamilton as partners, and Homer O'Dell as our manager. This was how the new dynamic team was born.

There were several wrestlers living at the Green Oak Apartments. Gene Anderson and his family, Juan Sebastian and his family, Larry Hamilton and his wife, all lived there. It was nice to have friends and their families close to us. Sometimes, we went to the pool, and Juan would be there with his little daughter. Gene

Anderson had an older daughter. They would be at the pool, too. We all got together and had a fun time. Also, there was a playground for the kids. That was Heather's favorite place. She liked to try to go to the playground by herself. She would hold one finger up and say, "Just one minute." Then, she started walking to the playground. We asked her, "Heather, where are you going?" She turned around and looked at us. She repeated, "Just one minute," and kept walking. Of course, we followed her to the playground.

*****

A large wrestling territory in North Carolina, South Carolina, Virginia, and West Virginia was operated from Charlotte. We had two or three towns running every night. One route we worked went like this. On Monday we started in Charlotte. On Tuesday some boys went to work High Point Television, some boys went to Raleigh, North Carolina for a house show, and some wrestled in Columbia, South Carolina. Then, after the television show, we went to Norfolk, Virginia for the Thursday night show. On Friday, we wrestled in Richmond. After Richmond, we went to Roanoke for the Saturday show. Then, we returned to Charlotte.

When I was in Charlotte, I had more free time. When I wrestled in Richmond on Friday, I took my family with me. There was a wonderful Chinese restaurant in Richmond. On Saturday, we drove to Roanoke. We stayed that night in Roanoke. On Sunday morning, we got up early to drive through the Blue Ridge Mountains.

There were many beautiful places to stop along our drive. The scenery was majestic. The air was crisp and cold. Even in the summer it stays cool in the mountains. We stopped at places we liked and had picnics. It was a relaxing and wonderful time. I did not worry about the business, because my obligation was only to wrestle.

Another route we wrestled was this. On Monday we were in Greensville, South Carolina. On Tuesday we worked High Point Television. It was Ashville, North Carolina on Wednesday. Then, we wrestled in Charleston, South Carolina on Thursday. During the summer, we wrestled at the ballpark in Florence, South Carolina. On Saturday we were in Lexington, South Carolina.

Then, on a different tour, we went all the way to Charleston, West Virginia for a Monday night show. On Tuesday we wrestled in Huntington, West Virginia. Then, we drove all the way back to Charlotte for television on Wednesday. Next, we went to Lumberton, North Carolina or Fayetteville, North Carolina. There were so many different towns to work in the North Carolina territory.

*****

Once I teamed up with Larry Hamilton and Homer O'Dell, we took turns driving each week. We always drove together, and we had fun. On Wednesday after we worked for Raleigh television, we drove to Norfolk for the Thursday night show. On the way to Norfolk, there was a small town with a great barbeque place. It was not a restaurant; it was a meat market. We knew the old couple who owned it. They liked it when the wrestlers came by the place. They would be making a large quantity of barbeque ribs. They cut us a few ribs each. They made their own special sauce. We enjoyed eating the North Carolina style barbeque ribs. They were delicious.

On Thursday, we wrestled in Norfolk, Virginia. There was a place called the Giant Supermarket where they would cook you a steak. We loved going to this market. Each of us picked out the largest steak, pork chops, or whatever meat we wanted that night. Then, for a few extra dollars, they cooked it for us right there. It was like a meat festival. We really enjoyed it.

Our team was getting hotter and hotter, because we were the worst boys in North Carolina. The people hated us. As usual, the more people hate us, the more they want to see us. We were happy about it. Every night, we were getting more money. We did our best to keep people hating us.

Richmond, Virginia was a hot town. The wrestling fans had a bad temper there. One night when we were wrestling, suddenly we heard a loud "bang!". Some crazy wrestling fan shot off his pistol. Fortunately, no one was injured. Many times the fans would get so hot they shot off their pistols in the air.

When we went to the wrestling shows, we would hide our car. If the wrestling fans knew our car, then they would throw stones to damage our car. We used to have somebody drive our car to a safe hiding place. After the match, the guy brought our car to us, and we drove out of the town secretly.

*****

The place where we were living, the Green Oak Apartments, was very convenient. It was close to downtown. Plus, it was easy to meet the other wrestlers, because the location was close to the highway.

We were happy living there. Heather was almost one year old. Hatsue was a great help to Judy with Heather, and she was learning English very well. Judy told me that when Hatsue, she, and Heather went shopping, people thought Heather was Hatsue's baby. Heather looked more Japanese than Caucasian. I was working as one of the top wrestlers in North Carolina territory; I was earning good money. My leisure time I spent with my family. We were enjoying our life in Charlotte, North Carolina.

*****

One week we were driving to Greenville, South Carolina for the Monday night match. We stopped by a drugstore. I saw a beautiful, big turtle stuffed toy. It fascinated me. I bought the turtle. Homer and Larry asked me what I was going to do with it. I told them it was a present for Heather. They laughed and said, "That turtle looks bigger than your baby." After the show, I brought it home for Heather. She was so happy. She loved her big turtle.

On Tuesday night, we wrestled in Columbia, South Carolina. The drive was about 90 miles from Charlotte. It was nice, because we did not have to leave too early. For some reason, Columbia was not drawing a good crowd no matter who was wrestling. We did not look forward to working in Columbia. The people were not interested in wrestling, and we did not make much money.

We went to Charleston, South Carolina for the Wednesday night show. I enjoyed being in Charleston. It was a seaport. Many of the houses had been built in the seventeenth and eighteenth centuries. There was a lot of history in that town.

That night, I wrestled with Larry Hamilton as partners and Homer O'Dell as our manager. Our opponents were the Amazing Zuma and Sailor Thomas. The Amazing Zuma was a guy from

Argentina. Sailor Thomas was a black guy from Milwaukee. He had an incredible physique. I had never seen anyone like him. He stood six feet and six inches tall, weighed 280 pounds, and had a 34 inch waist. He had a beautiful body.

Sailor Thomas' main hold was the bear hug. During the match, he threw his opponent against the ropes. After his opponent bounced off the ropes, then Sailor Thomas caught him in a bear hug. He was extremely strong. When we were wrestling that night, Sailor Thomas grabbed me, and threw me into the ropes. I hit the ropes as hard as I could, preparing to bounce off. The top rope broke. I fell to the floor. The boys watched me fall from the ring. Everyone thought I was dead. They told me I did about four somersaults before I hit the floor. I just lied on the floor frozen from shock. I checked my legs, my neck, everything. I could move, but I did not get up yet. Larry Hamilton came to my side and asked if I was okay. Larry and Homer took me to the dressing room. The match was over. Fortunately, I did not have one scratch. I was just dazed for a while.

After the match, we stopped by a supermarket called Piggly Wiggly. Larry said that they had good smoked carp. Where he came from by the Missouri River, he used to catch carp and then smoke it. I had eaten carp in Japan like sashimi, but I had never eaten it smoked. When I tasted it, the flavor was salty and delicious. Driving back to Charlotte, we ate smoked carp and drank beer all the way. We were having a great time.

That was another tour we worked. On Monday, we wrestled in Greenville, South Carolina. On Tuesday, we went to Columbia, South Carolina. On Wednesday, we were in Charleston, South Carolina. Then, on Thursday sometimes we went all the way back to Norfolk, Virginia, or we worked a spot show somewhere.

Other towns we wrestled in once a month were in West Virginia. On Monday we were in Charleston, West Virginia. We drove through the mountains. We took the West Virginia Turnpike to Charleston. It was about 320 miles. We left early to have enough time. Then, on Tuesday we worked in Huntington, West Virginia. After that show, we drove all the way to Raleigh for Wednesday night television.

One time when we were driving along the West Virginia Turnpike, there was a snow storm. The traffic was backed up for miles and miles. We were stuck on the highway for five hours in the cold weather. Finally, the traffic started moving. We left at about ten o'clock in the morning. We arrived in Raleigh at nine o'clock at night. It had been a long day stuck in the car. The television station knew we were going to be late, because of the snow.

In Charlotte we ran a show every Monday at a small place called Park Center in downtown. That place held about 1,500 people. Once a month, we booked a big show at The Coliseum. It was a new building. When the Coliseum first opened, we had an inauguration wrestling show. Homer O'Dell, Larry Hamilton, and I wrestled against George Bigcar, Johnny Weaver, and Sailor Thomas in a six man tag match. The place was sold out. There were 12,000 people at the Coliseum that night. Jim Crockett, Sr., our promoter was happy we had a sold out show on the first night.

*****

It was time for Hatsue to return to Japan. She had lived with us for six months. Her plane was scheduled to depart from Atlanta, Georgia. I drove her from Charlotte to Atlanta. I helped her to the plane. We said good-bye and she left. We were sad to part. We would miss each other very much. She had a wonderful time. Plus, she learned quite a good amount of English.

We lived in Charlotte for one year and four months. I wrestled all over North Carolina, South Carolina, Virginia, and West Virginia. Cowboy Luttrall called Jim Crockett, Sr. He needed me back in Florida. Judy and I packed our belongings again. We drove our two car convoy back to Tampa, Florida.

*****

Homer O'Dell, Larry Hamilton, and I came to Florida to work together. We started wrestling as a team in different cities. After a while, we were finished working together, and we went our separate ways. I stayed in Tampa. Homer and Larry went to Dallas, Texas. That was the last time I saw Homer O'Dell and Larry Hamilton.

I spoke to Larry about four years ago, in 1994 I believe. I was in Kansas City. I gave Larry a call. He said that it was great to hear from me, that it had been such a long time. We did not have an opportunity to see each other, but we promised one day we would. Unfortunately, Larry died two years ago from a heart attack.

I heard Homer O'Dell made good money from the wrestling business, but if Homer made $1,000 he spent $1,500. The problem was his spending. He ended up broke. The last I heard, he was driving a taxi in Nashville, Tennessee. He also passed away. Homer O'Dell was a character. He was absolutely fearless. One time he told me that in 1945 when he was in Japan during the American Occupation, he found a sack full of Japanese money. He had no idea what to do with it. He laughed. It was a joke to him. He found all this money and he did not know what to do, so he spent it all. I told him, "Boy! If I had found that money, I would be a millionaire, because I would have bought so much property in Japan." Homer was a big spender. Every year he had a brand new Cadillac. He did not care about tomorrow. He lived for today, having fun all the time.

19 FLORIDA 1969-1987
THE WRESTLING OFFICE
THE SPORTATORIUM
NATIONAL WRESTLING ALLIANCE

We came back to Florida in May or June 1969. We found an apartment. It was a brand new place. We lived there while we searched for a house. We looked for two months. Finally, we found a nice four bedroom house with a pool. It was perfect for us. Heather was about two years old at this time. We used to spend all day swimming and playing in the pool. We had so much fun. I have wonderful memories of that time.

After Homer O'Dell, Larry Hamilton, and I split up, I stopped wrestling every night. I participated in the promotion of Florida territory. I worked in the wrestling office. This gave me a schedule that allowed me to be at home more. I was enjoying my life with my family.

*****

That day in 1969 and 1970, the Florida wrestling office promoted in Puerto Rico for a show once a month. At this time, Masa Saito was wrestling in Florida. He and I teamed up. We flew to Puerto Rico to wrestle once a month. Usually the show was in San Fran on Saturday night. We left Tampa on Saturday morning, and we came back on Sunday morning.

I knew Puerto Rico since 1963. I had many memories come alive when I returned there in 1969. I had a great time wrestling in San Fran the first time. Plus, Judy and I went on our honeymoon there. I was delighted to go back to Puerto Rico once a month.

We arrived in San Fran around three o'clock in the afternoon. We checked into the airport hotel. It was convenient to stay there, because we had to leave in the morning. The wrestling shows were always packed. We had many wrestling fans in Puerto Rico.

After the show was over, I took Saito to one of the native restaurants to have dinner. We found a small bar after dinner. The place only had a counter where they sold beer and mondongo, a soup made with pig tripe. The flavor was delicious and spicy. Saito did not know what it was. I explained it to him. The soup was made with cow stomach or pig stomach. After a few beers, it tasted very good.

Another restaurant we liked was called Martin Firro. The cook was from Buenos Aires. They served Argentine style barbeque, all kinds of sausage and beef. The meat was cooked over a fire. We drank good wine and ate delicious barbeque. After the matches, we used to go there all the time. It was a favorite spot of ours. That was our enjoyment.

*****

In 1971, our wrestling office sponsored the Amateur Wrestling Tournament, the AU Tournament, in Tampa, Florida. For the AU Tournament, wrestlers from all over the United States competed in different wrestling divisions from light weight to heavy weight. I helped to organize the tournament to make sure everything ran smoothly.

One of the teams was the New York Athletic Club. Masao Hatori was representing this club for the 136 pound division. When I met Masao Hatori, he expressed his interest in opening a business with wrestling equipment. I did not know anything about this type of business, but I knew everything about wrestling. It seemed like a good idea; we could learn the business part of it. I was looking for some kind of venture so I agreed to invest money.

Masao Hatori moved to Florida. I started the Olympia Sunward Corporation. We opened a wrestling school. In those days, many people did not know about amateur wrestling. At this time, there were no high school wrestling teams. People heard about our school, and they became interested in the sport. After amateur wrestling became more popular, the high schools developed their own teams.

At Brandon High School, the coach did not know anything about wrestling. He brought his team to our wrestling school to learn from Masao. Also, the wrestling coach for a junior high school in Brandon brought his kids to us. These students eventually went on to Brandon High School to wrestle. Brandon High School developed one of the strongest wrestling teams because of Masao.

*****

Around 1973, Hatori introduced me to a guy named Shimura. Hatori and Shimura were on the same wrestling team in college. When Hatori was a senior, Shimura was a sophomore. After Shimura graduated, he wanted to learn English. He came to the United States. He traveled all over America by bus. He came to visit Hatori in Florida.

When I met him, he told me he had experience in the fishing business. His intention was to return to Japan and start a tuna business. He asked me if I wanted to be involved. It sounded like a good business, so I invested money into it.

In 1973, I drove from Florida to Maine and to Prince Edward Island. I bought yellowfin and bluefin tuna. Then, I shipped the tuna to Japan by Japan Airlines or Flying Tiger Cargo. I did not make money. I lost money, but it was a great experience. I traveled to Maine and to Prince Edward Island. Then, I drove to Logan Airport in Boston to ship the cargo.

When I started the business, Judy's brother Terry, wanted to join me. He was tired of his work. He helped me with the business. Even though we lost money, we had an adventure. We tried something new.

Heather, Stephanie, and Judy went with me during my first trip up north. We spent a few days in Portland, Maine. Then, my family went back to Tampa and I stayed in Maine. The business base was in Portland. From there, I traveled across through St. John, cross the Canadian border, to Moncton, and to Prince Edward Island. On my visit to Prince Edward Island, I could not believe it. It was a fishing village about 200 years old. It seemed like it had not changed for all that time. I was surprised.

Once I went to a place called Tignish on Prince Edward Island. It was on the left side way up on the tip of the island. The houses must have been about 200 years old. The houses were country, rustic style. From there, I could see all of the Atlantic to the Georgia bank. The wind was icy cold. I have a vivid picture in my mind of this place. It was beautiful.

In Portland, Maine our contact was a guy named Charlie Chee. He was a Korean man who owned a company called Global Fishery. Also, another guy named Gordon Hurtchbig who owned a shrimp business worked with us. These guys were helping us produce the tuna business.

When I was on Prince Edward Island, I went to the capital called Charlottetown. That day I had nothing to do, so I was just driving around downtown. I was going to eat lunch at a good Chinese restaurant. I stopped at a red light waiting for it to change. I watched as three girls crossed in front of me. They looked Japanese. I was fascinated that three Japanese girls were in front of me. I thought to myself, "What are they doing on Prince Edward Island?" To be sure, I asked them, "Are you Japanese? They said, "Yes, we are." I asked them what they were doing there. They told me they were tourists. They had a friend who married a Canadian man. They came to visit her and to sight see. I invited the girls to have lunch with me at the Chinese restaurant. They were delighted to join me.

At the restaurant, I ordered a round of beers. We said, "Kampai!" toasting to each other. We shared stories. We had a great time. It was nice to be with Japanese people again. I drove them to their girlfriend's house. I dropped them off. We said good-bye, and I went on my way.

I never thought I would see those girls again. In 1975, I went back to Japan as the Junior Heavyweight Champion. There was a big show in Tokyo. When I was in my dressing room, I was told three girls were waiting to see me. I was surprised. I went to see who they could be. I saw the three girls from Prince Edward Island in front of me. I could not believe it. When they heard I was going to be wrestling In Tokyo, they came to the show. They brought flowers to me. I was delighted to see them again. After this we kept in touch, corresponding about once a year around the holiday time.

In the tuna business, we bought about 800 pounds of tuna. Sometimes from Canada we transferred the tuna to Maine where we were based. It was packed in ice. We drove to Logan Airport in

Boston, and the tuna was shipped to Japan. That tuna went to the Tsukiji Fish Market.

Who thought I would go into the tuna business? I was foolish. I was looking for a venture. I wanted to make more money. It was greed. I was told it was a great business. I had plenty of money in the wrestling business, so I had money to invest. I learned the hard way, the school of hard knocks. Only failure can make a good businessman. If you are successful at everything, then you do not learn anything. You don't know what failure is. That is why it is called "the school of hard knocks".

The tuna season was only two months, August and September. After those months, I returned to Tampa. I continued with the wrestling business. In 1973 and 1974, I wrestled once or twice a week. The rest of the time I stayed in the office, participating in the wrestling promotions.

*****

Back in 1972, I wrestled two to three times a week in Florida. The rest of the time I stayed in the office. The Georgia territory had its office in Atlanta. There was a wrestling war going on there. Buddy Fuller and Ray Gunkel split, and they went against each other. Buddy Fuller was a partner with us in Florida; therefore, we went to help his company. A good friend of mine from Oklahoma, Bill Watts, was the booker for Buddy. I used to fly to Atlanta every Friday. I stayed Friday, Saturday, and Sunday. Then, I returned to Florida on Monday. I made that trip every week for three months. I enjoyed getting out of Florida to work a different territory.

In 1964, I had a good experience in Atlanta wrestling for the Junior Heavyweight Championship. I liked the city very much. It was nice to be working in Atlanta again. This time when I was working there on the weekends, I stayed with Bill Watts at his apartment.

After the wrestling war was resolved, Bill Watts came to Florida to be a booker in 1973. He stayed for one year. Then, he went to Oklahoma to become partners with Leroy McGuirk. In 1975, Oklahoma needed to book good talent. Bill asked me to work for him. I accepted his offer, and I went back on the road in Oklahoma. I spent ten months traveling to all the different places I knew. I came home to Florida once a month. Then, I returned to Oklahoma and Louisiana. In 1976, I finished working for Bill Watts, and I went home to Florida.

When I went to Oklahoma in 1975, it had been eleven years since I wrestled there in 1964. The promotion had changed since Bill Watts bought into the business with Leroy McGuirk. Bill wanted to expand to many different cities. He tried pushing the business in many directions. Some towns drew a crowd and some did not draw. It did not feel the same as I remembered. Also, in 1962 and in 1964 when I was there, I had a more enthusiastic mind. Everything was new to me back then. Now, I already knew the places; I was not as excited. I was there to help a friend. I did not have a challenge though. It was nice to get away from Florida, to hit the road, and to see old friends like Dick Murdoch and Killer Karl Kox. I was working with my old buddies. Also, it was good to see Heime Vimer again. He was happy to see me again, too.

I finished working in Oklahoma in the middle of 1976. I returned to Florida. Judy and I bought a large property on a lake, Lake Carroll. We were preparing the plans to build a beautiful house for our family.

Before we built our house, we used to go to the lake property and stay for a couple days. We put a mobile trailer on the property for our temporary house. We enjoyed swimming in the lake. Also, I built a dock. When the Japanese wrestlers were in Florida, they helped me. We put in the posts and placed the lumber across it for the deck. It was 30 feet long. It was hard work, but it was worth it. Plus, it was an extra work out for the boys. We enjoyed taking sun on the dock. Heather and Stephanie liked to swim in the water. We had a great time on the lake property.

*****

While I was working in the wrestling office, I only wrestled two to three times a week. If one of the wrestlers could not make the show, then I would substitute for him. My main focus was the business. I enjoyed the schedule. I spent most of my time at home with my family after office hours.

The office was located at the Sportatorium. We had a gym behind the office. We used to shoot the television wrestling shows there. The television show was only once a week, so we had plenty of time to utilize the facility. There were many young boys from all over the United States who came to our office to become professional wrestlers. They knew the reputation of Hiro Matsuda, and they wanted to learn from the best. I participated mostly in the training of new talent. For example, I trained Mike Graham, the son of Eddie Graham. Also, I trained Steve Keirn. The most famous wrestler I trained was Hulk Hogan. I think that was in 1978 or 1979.

His name was Terry Bollea when I first met him. He was playing in a musical band in Tampa. He was a nice looking, big boy. He came to the wrestling office. He said he wanted to become a professional wrestler. I told him, "I will give you the opportunity, if you can keep up with me." He agreed, "Yes, I will keep up with you, Mr. Matsuda." He was one of my proteges.

In the meantime, another guy named Paul Orndorff came to me. He was a great college football player. Now, he wanted to become a professional wrestler. Then, another boy named Brian Blair showed up to be trained. I had three boys at once to train, Terry, Paul, and Brian.

I spent every morning five days a week training those boys. They showed great potential, because they could keep up with me. Sometimes, they had a hard time, but they never said that they could not continue. They tried their best to keep up. I was twice as old as they were. I kept telling them, "Keep up with me!" If they could not, they would feel very ashamed. Therefore, they kept up with me very well.

In order to become a good wrestler, you had to have it in you from the heart. It is easy to become a professional wrestler, but if you want to work the main event, then you must have guts and determination. In order to make determination, you have to go through the grind mill to build endurance. Also, your mind has to be very strong. I gave those boys a great opportunity, not just the physical training but the mental training, too. After four months of intensive training, they passed my test. I started showing them wrestling moves in the ring. The best way to learn professional wrestling is to work in front of the public. If you make a mistake, you correct it the next day.

Those three boys had great determination. They started in Florida. In the beginning, a wrestler earns enough money to eat. He would go from one territory to another to work. The learning experience was on the road. That way a wrestler learns from experience. After two or three years, those boys made it to the top all over the United States. Terry became Hulk Hogan, the most famous wrestler in the entire United States. Paul went to New York and became Mr. Wonderful Paul Orndorff. Brian Blair did it the same way. All three were top wrestlers working the main events.

There was another boy named Ray Fernandez who came to me for training. Ray's father was a deputy sheriff of Hillsborough County. He came to the Sportatorium to ask for his son to become a professional wrestler. He was told to bring Ray to me. The office said to him, "Hiro Matsuda will give your son the opportunity, but only if the boy can endure the training." His father brought Ray to me. Ray Fernandez looked great. He weighed 230 pounds, and he had a nice physique. He went through the hard training and he made it. He was also one of the top wrestlers in the United States.

My idea was to discourage the boys so they would quit. I worked the boys hard to see if they had the determination and the guts to be a great wrestler. Without this, there was no way to make it to the top. Many boys came to the Sportatorium. Maybe 20 guys showed up and only one survived. That guy had heart to make it big in the business. No matter how famous the boys I trained became, they showed their appreciation of what I gave to them. When they thanked me, that was my satisfaction.

*****

The gym behind the wrestling office at the Sportatorium was known as the "Snake Pit" by all the wrestlers. The reputation grew from the story that once the boys got in the ring with Hiro Matsuda, they could not get out without his permission. If a boy wanted to become a professional wrestler at the top of the business, then he had to go to Tampa and take instruction from Hiro Matsuda. This was my reputation all over the United States.

In those days there were many wrestling schools. They knew nothing about wrestling. They charged so much money and gave some instruction. It was a rip off. At the Tampa Sportatorium, I did not have a wrestling school. I only accepted the disciplined boys. It was not a business. I did my best to discourage the boys. Only if the boys had heart and discipline did I allow them to train with me. I never charged money, because I was not in the training business to make money. I was looking for good talent. Most of the boys who wanted to become professional wrestlers did not have much money anyway. How would they even be able to pay for training? Sometimes, I spent money on those boys. I gave them some extra dollars if they needed something. Also, since I did not take any money for their training, I could drive them as hard as I needed. Then, if they could not keep up with me, I could kick them out. But if they could endure the training, then I knew they would be great wrestlers.

*****

As I mentioned earlier in my story, there were many wrestling territories. Florida office ran the entire Florida territory. Georgia office ran the Georgia territory. Jim Crockett in North Carolina ran three different states. Nick Gulas and Roy Welch ran the Tennessee and the Kentucky territory. Alabama and parts of Mississippi were one territory. Leroy McGuirk and Bill Watts ran Oklahoma, Louisiana, and Arkansas. Amarillo, West Texas was ran by Dory Funk, Sr. Dallas, Texas was ran by Fritz Von Erich. Kansas City and Minneapolis were territories. There were so many territories in those days, we called the business the National Wrestling Alliance, NWA. Each territory respected the boundaries.

Around 1980, Vince McMahon, Sr. died. Vince McMahon, Sr. of the New York office had a good relationship with the Florida wrestling office, because Eddie Graham used to work for Vince in 1957 and 1958. When Vince McMahon, Sr. died, his son Vince McMahon, Jr. took over the New York wrestling office. He had great marketing ability. He was in a different entertainment business. Vince, Jr. utilized a Madison Avenue advertising agency. The New York office expanded television programming all over the United States. Very soon, with the television advertising revenue, he could spend more money than any other promoter who belonged to the NWA. Therefore, Vince, Jr. expanded his business all over the United States.

The boys who worked for the different territories for the main event realized the potential of earning big money with Vince, Jr. Most of the top wrestlers in other territories went to New York to work for Vince, Jr. Soon he took over the entire United States on his own, because the smaller territories could not compete. Without the top talent, there was no way to draw the wrestling fans.

Vince, Jr. did not come into all of Florida. He only went to Miami. In the meantime, North Carolina territory was putting up a fight to compete with Vince, Jr. Jim Crockett, Jr. had a big ego. He bought the Georgia territory. Then, he bought the Louisiana and Oklahoma territory. His ego was so big, he forgot about his friendships. When Jim Crockett, Sr. was alive, we used to work closely with him. His son had no respect for any business relationship, so he began pushing his wrestling promotions into Florida trying to take over the territory.

The Florida territory was doing great business, but eventually this slowed down. The wrestling office began having trouble. Before 1985, Eddie Graham extended his business affairs. He invested a lot of money into a real estate deal that was bigger than what he could handle. He started having financial problems. His mental attitude was not as sharp as it had once been. He had a genius mind for running the wrestling business, but he had too many personal financial troubles. His investments were going sour, and his mind was clouded with worry. He neglected running the wrestling business which had earned him the most of his money in the first place. He forgot about his roots.

I only had ten percent of the company. I did not have a big voice when problems came up in the office. I stayed away from the wrestling office instead of facing the hardship. We were all good friends in the business. We shared in a successful business for many years. It was difficult to discuss the problems. Friends did not want to step on each other's toes. No one brought up the business trouble; everyone looked the other way. I did not feel I could say anything with my small percentage. It was frustrating. It was easier to just stay away.

*****

In 1985, Eddie Graham suffered a nervous breakdown. He committed suicide. Duke called me. He said, "Eddie killed himself!" I rushed to Duke's house. Duke and I went to Eddie's house. Already, his body was being carried to the hospital in the ambulance.

By the time it arrived at St. Joseph's Hospital, he was announced dead.

After Eddie's death, I found out more details about the problems he had. He and a partner invested money in a real estate deal. His partner was a con artist. Eddie took the responsibility for the deal. He signed a bank note for one million dollars. His partner went bankrupt. The real estate deal did not go through. Now, it was Eddie's responsibility to pay back the one million dollars. After that, his only concern was how he was going to pay back one million dollars. It drove him nuts. He consumed alcohol and valium. His mind was always somewhere else. I saw him one time in his office sitting in the dark staring at the wall. He did not see me. That was the state of his mind. It did not take long for him to break down.

Duke explained to me that one day Eddie confided in him about the pressure he had. Eddie had to come up with $650 a day just for the interest payment. His greed had blinded him. He went into business with a crook, and Eddie took the entire responsibility for it.

*****

Dusty Rhodes was a partner in the Florida wrestling company. Eddie gave him five percent. He had a great, creative mind. Dusty was the booker for the territory. He also had an ego bigger than an elephant. He told Eddie he wanted to go to North Carolina as a booker. Eddie gave him permission to go. He went to work for Jim Crockett, Jr., the other egomaniac. Together, they tried to come into the Florida territory. They were slowly pushing in little by little. I suppose they had a small amount of conscience, because they did not come in all the way.

*****

There was a guy named Lester Welch. He was a friend of Eddie's. In the past he was a partner with our corporation, but later on he sold his shares and moved to Georgia. He had filed bankruptcy about three or four times. I did not know the relationship between Eddie and Lester. Eddie brought him back to Florida. Lester ran spot shows. He found towns to run a show in once a month or once every three months. That was all he was doing, but Eddie gave him six percent of the gross. No matter if he drew people or not, Lester still made money. I asked Mike, Eddie's son, what was the relationship between Eddie and Lester. He did not even understand it. Lester was draining the company's finances. This was another incident I could not comprehend.

*****

In 1985 after Eddie died, the company held a meeting. No one wanted to pick up the responsibility of running the business. Mike, Eddie's son, would like to have taken over, but he did not know the wrestling business. At this time, I had my own business called Olympia Sunward Corporation, a sporting goods business. I learned business through the school of hard knocks. I owned ten percent of the wrestling business. I volunteered to take charge of the company. I cared about this business, and I did not want to see it disintegrate. Duke helped in the office all the time, but his personality could not take the heat of the wrestlers complaining. I did not mind taking the heat. I would explain to the boys the way the business was going. If they did not like it, they were free to leave.

When I took over the business, I did not take the title of president. I did not want to carry that title, but I was running the company. The first thing I had to do was review the financial report. The company was $150,000 in the red. I had to find places to cut our expenses.

The first thing I did was cut Lester Welch off. I brought in Danny Miller from the Carolinas. He used to promote Greenville, South Carolina and some spot shows. He was mistreated by Jim Crockett, Jr. When I called him, he was delighted to come down to Florida. He replaced Lester Welch. We made a deal. Danny was not satisfied with what I could pay him, but he agreed anyway. Now, I had a right hand man I could trust.

Wahoo McDaniel was our booker. He wrestled and he received money for a booking fee. He was not drawing the amount he was supposed to be drawing, so I showed him the books. I told him, "You are getting this much money, but you do not bring in enough money to pay the expenses." He was a good friend of mine. We discussed the situation. Finally, he decided to leave. We split on good terms. I brought in my man Bob Roop as the booker.

I paid off the $150,000 in three months. I cut here and there; then, I brought in enough money to pay the debt. In the meantime, I produced three of my top new talent. I trained Lex Luger, Ed "The Bull" Gantner, and Ron Simmons.

Larry Pfohl became Lex Luger. He went to the University of Miami where he played football. He also played professional football. One day, he came to the wrestling office. He said he wanted to become a professional wrestler. The next day I met him. I told him exactly how he had to take my training. Somehow he had prepared himself. He had heard about how I trained boys. The first day he kept up with me. I was very surprised. He had so much determination.

Larry had a friend named Ed Gantner. He played football at Central Florida University. Then, he played professional football for the Tampa Bay Bandits. Larry brought him to try out. Ed passed my training test.

Ron Simmons was also a Tampa Bay Bandits football player. Since the team went bankrupt, he was looking for something else. He wanted to become a professional wrestler.

I trained these three boys at the same time. I needed wrestlers who could draw money. The first guy was Larry Pfohl. We had been talking about what his wrestling name should be. He came up with Lex Luger, luger like a German pistol. I thought it was an excellent name. I taught him everything I knew about wrestling, so he could respond right away and draw money. For four months I sat ringside. I told him every move to make. For the first match, we went to Ocean City in Daytona. He wrestled against Cocoa Samoa. I was more nervous than Lex Luger was, but he went successfully for ten minutes. The crowd responded beautifully. I knew this guy would draw.

Before Wahoo McDaniel left the business, he had four weeks to work. He wrestled against Lex Luger at the Bayfront Center in St. Petersburg. I did not expect a big crowd, because Lex Luger was new. He surprised everybody, especially me. Lex Luger became the star of Florida.

I told Ed Gantner "You have to wrestle like a bull." His name became Ed "The Bull" Gantner. He was a hell of a guy, an easy-going guy. Unfortunately, he had a steroid problem, and no one knew about it. He went through college and professional football.

His kidneys were shot from the use of steroids. He was devastated, because he could not wrestle anymore. Later, I found out he shot himself. Ed "The Bull" was a hell of a guy. I was so sorry to hear what happened to him.

Barry Windham was another hot young wrestler. I knew his father. Barry started wrestling when he was sixteen years old. Barry was getting a guarantee from the Florida wrestling office when Eddie was in charge. When I took over, we could not afford to give a guarantee. I called Barry into the office. I told him, "Unfortunately, the company cannot afford to pay you a guarantee. I can only pay you a percentage of what you draw. If you draw, then I will pay you what you are worth." He was a gentleman. He agreed.

*****

The Florida wrestling company did very well in 1986 with the new talent. We paid the bills and all of the debt. However, Jim Crockett, Jr. and Dusty Rhodes were still trying to expand all over the country competing with Vince McMahon, Jr. They offered Lex Luger, Ed "The Bull" Gantner, and Barry Windham big guarantees. Lex Luger came to my house to talk to me. He said, "Mr. Matsuda, North Carolina territory has promised me big money." I could not tell him, "No, you cannot leave." If I were in his shoes, I would take the offer, too. That is how professional wrestlers are. You want to make money. I told him, "Fine. Just give me four weeks to prepare someone to take your place." Then, Barry Windham was in the same situation.

The North Carolina territory was stealing our talent. Without top talent, our business was slowly going down. North Carolina forced us to join their territory. That was in 1987. We could not continue alone anymore. I could create new talents, buy once they were at the top, North Carolina would steal them. Therefore, Wahoo, Dusty, Jim, and his brother David Crockett came down to Florida. We negotiated a deal. They offered to buy the Florida territory. Looking back now I wish I had sold it, but at that time, my heart was into reviving the business and the territory. I did not want to sell it.

We agreed that the North Carolina office would do the booking for the Florida territory. They had all of our top talent; however, they did not book any of the good wrestlers for the Florida shows. Naturally, our shows did not draw, and we made little money. We also did joint venture shows in Orlando and Miami. Of course, these were sold out shows. We used all of the top wrestlers. After these big shows, North Carolina kept Lex Luger and Ed "The Bull" Gantner working in its territory. They were sending me boys I had never heard of before. How could I draw a crowd in different cities with no name wrestlers? Jim Crockett, Jr. was planning to run our business into the ground and then take over.

The North Carolina promotions spent big money on the wrestlers. They owned two leer jets. It looked great on the surface, but their financial status was not stable. They were spending more money than they were earning.

We had a great show in Gainesville and in Miami. After the match was over, they were supposed to send us a portion of the revenue. The week we were supposed to receive our money, they did not send it to us. I did not have money to pay the employees. They paid the wrestlers, but I had office employees that needed to be paid. Also, our office had its own expenses to cover.

Danny Miller, my right hand man, took care of the Miami and the Gainesville shows. He brought the checks back from the show; then, we were expected to send the money to the North Carolina office. I had another plan. When I went to the office the next morning, I asked for the checks. I was told they were on route to North Carolina by Federal Express already. I was so angry. If we sent that money to North Carolina, then we would never see a dime, and our bills and employees would not get paid. I called Federal Express to track the package and send it back to us. When I received the checks, I deposited them into our account. I paid our expenses and the employees.

The North Carolina office did not say one word to me about the money. They knew they had been wrong not to pay our office. They knew me and how I would react. I did not hear anything from them about the situation. That was the end of the relationship between the Florida territory and the North Carolina territory. We could not continue to operate our office. We closed the business. It was 1987. I did the best that I could to keep the business alive. Unfortunately, the timing and the circumstances were not right for us.

The North Carolina office had to close down, too. They were drawing a good house at each show, but they mismanaged their finances. They spent too much money. Jim Crockett, Sr. spent 50 years building his reputation in the wrestling business. He established North Carolina as a strong territory. He earned a fortune with his wrestling promotions. He was a wonderful man. His son ruined his reputation, and he ran the business into the ground. It is a shame it happened that way.

20 ATLANTA

Jim Barnett was a friend of mine, a promoter for Georgia. He knew Ted Turner very well. Turner Broadcasting was looking for programs. Turner Broadcasting had been carrying wrestling for many years. They did not want to lose the program. The ratings were great. When North Carolina had to close due to financial trouble, Turner bought Jim Crockett Promotions.

I believe it was 1988 or 1989, a good friend of mine, George Scott, was the first booker for WCW, the World Championship Wrestling at Turner Broadcasting. He asked me to work for WCW as a manager for Rick Flair. They offered me good money, so I accepted the position. However, because of the past struggles in the wrestling business, many guys were still fighting for control of the business. George Scott had brilliant ideas and experience, but the other guys got together to kick him out of the business. Finally, they succeeded. George called me and told me what happened. When George left the company, I decided to leave, too. I worked there for about four months. I had a great time. If they had kept George Scott, the business would have expanded quickly and successfully.

*****

When Turner Broadcasting bought Jim Crockett Promotions, Jack Petrik was in charge of the company. He was the executive of Turner Broadcasting. He hired Jim Herd. I heard he used to run a pizza business. How in the hell is a guy who ran a pizza business going to know how to run the wrestling business?

Jim Barnett was running Georgia before Jim Crockett, Jr. bought the territory. Now, he was the advisor to Jim Herd. Also, he was working for Turner Broadcasting wrestling division. One day, Jim called me. He said "Hiro, I have a guy. His name is Jorge Gonzalez. He is seven feet and four inches tall; he weighs 450 pounds. He is from Argentina. He tried to make the Atlanta Hawks basketball team. He was on the national basketball team in Argentina. Turner Broadcasting wants to break him into the wrestling business. Would you like to train him?" I did not mind training him. We made arrangements for Jorge to come to Tampa to train.

The first thing I had to do was put some muscle on him. Basketball players do not need weight, but wrestlers need muscle. Jorge had a great size, but he needed more muscle. I took him to Gold's Gym for weight training. After he gained some muscle, I took him to the Sportatorium to teach him wrestling.

His heart was not in the wrestling business. The reason he was in the business was his size. He knew no one had his size, so he thought he was already a star. I did not care what he thought. It was my job to get him into shape for wrestling. If he was my boy, I would have kicked him out the door the first day, but Jim asked me to train him. We made a deal.

Jorge was a good kid. He had a good nature. However, to become a professional wrestler, he needed more discipline. He was a quick learner, though. He had to realize that size meant nothing. A large size is good at first appearance, but if he did not have knowledge of wrestling, the people could see through him. He would not keep the attention of the wrestling fans if he could not perform well. The size meant nothing. I tried to tell him this, but he did not get it.

*****

When Jorge was training, I had a helper, David Sierra. I could not take Jorge everywhere. David was another wrestler. I was fortunate to have a helper. One day, Jorge was complaining of a stomach ache. We thought he had the flu. His symptoms seemed like the flu. His pain did not go away. We rushed him to the walk-in-clinic. They told us to take him to the emergency room immediately.

At the hospital, he was diagnosed with pancreatitis. He was put in intensive care for one week. Fortunately, he was working for Turner

Broadcasting, because he was covered by medical insurance. I called Jim Herd to tell him what happened. He flew to Tampa to visit Jorge in the hospital. The bill was over $50,000. He was lucky to be with Turner Broadcasting. If he was not, he would have dropped dead in the street. They gave him a $350,000 guarantee without even wrestling yet. No wonder he thought he was a star.

*****

Jorge traveled to different places to wrestle for the WCW. He did not draw the crowds. His contract was for one year. Turner Broadcasting realized he could not draw the people. Vince McMahon, Jr. wanted a big guy. Jorge left the WCW, and he went to New York to work for the WWF. Vince, Jr. learned from his father not to give wrestlers a guarantee. Jorge asked Vince, Jr. for a guarantee, but Vince said he could not give a big guarantee. He offered him only the minimum and a percentage of the house Jorge drew. Jorge started to learn the hard way. The New York office used him for a few months; then, they cut him loose. If he had taken my advice, followed my instruction, he could have stayed longer in the wrestling business. Now, he went back to Argentina. I do not know what he is doing now. He did save every nickel he made. I think he is well off in Argentina.

*****

It was 1990. I was working on and off with the WCW. When they needed me, they called me. My good friend, Masa Saito, was the American wrestling coordinator for New Japan Pro Wrestling. I used to send boys to New Japan Pro Wrestling when Sakaguchi was the booker in 1986. After that time, I did not work for them. When Saito became in charge of the American wrestlers, he came to see me in Atlanta when I had business with the WCW. I made a meeting for both companies. We made arrangements to work together.

Since then, I have been working with New Japan Pro Wrestling. For the first Tokyo Dome show, I made the deal. I took the top WCW wrestlers. We sold out the Tokyo Dome. Lex Luger and the Steiner brothers made a sensational performance. Overnight, they became stars in Japan. This was my new career. WCW liked to have the Japanese boys, like The Great Muta and Sasaki, once in a while. I was working with a guy named Bill Bush at the WCW office. He was working as the financial controller. He applied for the visas for the boys. I became very acquainted with Bill. When the office wanted Japanese boys, he made arrangements. When the boys came to the United States, I accompanied them to different cities. I really enjoyed seeing the cities where I had once wrestled. Also, traveling on the road felt good. It was a nice time.

*****

There is a hotel called The Days Inn in Atlanta by Highway 285. The manager's name was DeLaney. I used to know her a long time ago. She used to be the manager of a hotel near the airport a few years back. Most of the boys stayed at The Days Inn near the airport near Highway 285. When I went there, I saw DeLaney; I had not seen her in years. Every time I went to Atlanta, I went to a place where they knew me. I enjoyed it. There was a nice country bar downstairs at the hotel. At night time, Dick Murdoch, my friend who was also working for Atlanta, and I met at the bar sometimes when we got off early. DeLaney came by after work, too. We sat together, and we talked about the old days. I knew DeLaney from 1972. She was the manager of the Royal Hotel at the airport where I used to stay. Dick Murdoch was younger. He was working for the WCW when I was sending the Japanese boys to the WCW. Once in a while I saw him at The Days Inn. We had a few beers, talked about old times, listened to country music. We enjoyed the companionship. The bar closed at 2:30 in the morning. After closing, we went to the Waffle House on the corner for breakfast. It was like the old days.

*****

This is another story about when I was working with the WCW. Before the Tokyo Dome show, I went ahead of the WCW members to Japan. I had to make arrangements. At the end of the year, every company had a closing party. New Japan Pro Wrestling invited me to its party. I saw a friend of mine there. His name was Misawa. I had not seen Misawa in many years. It had been almost 20 years. He said he was working with the merchandising for New Japan Pro

Wrestling. We were talking. He showed me samples. They were not what I expected. Jokingly I said, "I can make you better merchandise than this." Misawa got serious then. He was interested in how I could do that.

That is how I started Matsuda Enterprises. I started sending merchandise to the Tokyo Dome shows. I created different T-shirts with beautiful designs of the wrestlers. The shirts were very popular. One year I sold over 40,000 T-shirts. I had three years of successful business. I worked with the company until the president of the company passed away from an aneurysm. Misawa was the vice president. Now, there was a power struggle. Another president took over the company. That was the end of the merchandise business.

21 WORLD SUPERSTAR WRESTLING

In 1993 I started another business called World Superstar Wrestling, Incorporated. I had a contract with TV Asahi. They supplied me with New Japan Pro Wrestling video tapes. We had a 50% - 50% deal. If I made a profit, TV Asahi got 50%. After I received the raw footage of the wrestling shows, I had the tapes edited to create my own show.

Heather was in Tampa at the time. She was working for West Advertising Company. She had connections with West End Recording. The owner was Tim Shapiro. The other company was Cypress Production Company where we did the tape editing. A guy named Paul Berkowitz was the expert on editing. Heather introduced me to Tim and Paul. They were the right men I had been waiting to meet.

Paul made the edit for the demonstration tape to take to MIPCOM for the television presentation. MIPCOM is a television and movie promotional convention held every year. People from all over come to MIPCOM. Production companies, movie companies, all entertainment companies are assembled in Cannes, France to display their merchandise to attract buyers from all over the world. It is usually held for five days.

Howard Brody became my partner. He had 10% of the company. He had a friend in New York who had been participating in MIPCOM every year. He represented children's programs. He asked Howard to share a booth with him, so we could split the cost. We agreed and paid our share. Howard's friend introduced us to the MIPCOM Organization. That is how we went to our first MIPCOM. We were the blind leading the blind. I thought Howard knew more about television marketing, but he was as blind like I was.

He has a natural talent for talking with people. He has a golden tongue.

We made a nice brochure. Paul created a wonderful five minute demonstration tape. I made a poster with the Great Muta, Jushin Liger, the top boys working for New Japan Pro Wrestling. We had the brochure, the poster, and the demo tape. We went to Cannes, France. We were nervous in the beginning, but after the first day, we were fine. Most people who came from different countries were very interested. They had seen the WWF/WWE and the WCW in the past. They did not know another wrestling company existed.

Turner Broadcasting had a big display booth. They represented many movies and television shows. WCW was one of its programs.

Howard made a few contacts, Italy, Turkey, five or six different countries. At the end of MIPCOM, Howard calculated he had almost $350,000 sales on paper. I told him the paper was only an interested promise; we had no contracts. We would not know until the follow-up. Once the contract is signed, payment is made, then I believe it. On paper, you can write a million dollars, but it means nothing. Howard was still excited though. It was the first time he had seen $350,000, even if it was only on paper.

*****

We entered our application late, so we could not get a hotel close to the convention hall. Our hotel was an old building overlooking the hillside. Old people ran the place. We had to walk about ten minutes to the exhibition hall. Every morning, we went downstairs to a small restaurant for breakfast which was included in the room fee. After breakfast, we packed up, dressed in our suits, and went to the convention. We walked through the streets seeing many different things. The streets were lined with expensive stores and many restaurants. We took a different route every day. We searched for where we would have dinner that night as we walked. We arrived at the exhibition hall at eight-thirty in the morning. The show started at nine.

When we got to the exhibition hall, Howard's friend started introducing us to many buyers. Soon we started meeting the exhibitioners and their products. We became very acquainted. We met people from all over the world. They were doing the same thing as us, trying to sell their products.

The first day, we were just getting our feet wet. We did not have time to relax, because we were tense from so many buyers coming to our booth. We did not know the procedure. That night when we returned to the hotel, we each took a hot shower and freshened-up. We decided where we would eat dinner. There were many small, family restaurants close to our hotel. We walked around and on the corner, we found a cozy restaurant with a bar. We went in, tried to speak a little broken French. The people were nice. I ordered a veal cutlet, spaghetti, and a beer called "1664", one of my favorites. We had a nice evening. We had a delicious dinner in a cozy, warm atmosphere. It was a wonderful time. On the way back to our hotel, the stores were closed so we were window shopping. Then, we returned to the hotel and settled down to have a good night sleep in Cannes, France.

The second day, we were much more comfortable, because we knew the atmosphere. Also, we knew the procedure and how to deal with people. I let Howard talk to most of the clients. I introduced the customers to my sales director, Howard. He did very well. He met with many potential buyers from other countries. They talked like they would buy from us, but when Howard made the follow up most said they could not make a deal. Many of the exhibitioners were in the same situation. Promises. Promises. Really there is a small percentage of people who buy the product.

The exhibition was open until seven o'clock in the evening. Everyone took a lunch break from twelve to twelve-thirty in the afternoon. Cannes is the Riviera Beach. There are restaurants all over. Our enjoyment was going to different restaurants for lunch, have wine or beer, and good food. The food was so great no matter where we went. If we did not have time for lunch, there was always a coffee shop. They served sandwiches, beer, wine, whiskey, anything you wanted. Also, the vendors pushed carts with drinks and food. They came to your booth. Most people came back around three o'clock in the afternoon. The most busy time was from ten in the morning to twelve in the afternoon. The late afternoon was slower than the morning. The majority of the people left the place around five. We stayed until seven, the closing time.

The second night we found a neighborhood restaurant across the street from our hotel. We went in, and no one spoke English. Fortunately, one lady spoke Spanish. She was working there from Spain. I spoke Spanish to order our food. We ate excellent food and drank wine to celebrate our time at Cannes MIPCOM.

The third night, not too far from the hotel, we found a nice native restaurant. They served fish mostly, but also some pork and lamb. The menu was written in French, not English so we had difficulty ordering. I wanted fish which is poisson, but it came out sounding like passion. It sounded like I said, "I want passion." The lady turned red, and looked at me strangely. I corrected myself. We laughed and laughed. She understood. She explained to me what it would be in French correctly. I have had many experiences going to different countries and not speaking the language, but somehow I managed to order food. The food was delicious. When we left our waitress laughed at us. It was a good experience, reminded me of when I was in Mexico and South America. I did not speak Spanish at that time. Now, trying to order food in French brought back memories.

About three streets over from our hotel was the beach street along the Riviera. There were many restaurants lining the beach, but those restaurants cater to the tourists. Everyone speaks English. A few blocks behind the beach, there were restaurants where the natives go. Those are the places I enjoy because of the atmosphere. Also, I like to mingle with the native people even though I do not speak French, I can try to converse with people. I am very good at picking up language quickly. If I stayed there two or three months, I could get by with the language.

*****

In 1993 World Superstar Wrestling did not have an income yet. We were still building our business. Matsuda Enterprises loaned money to the new company to cover the expenses of MIPCOM. Matsuda Enterprises got the benefit of a tax write-off. It worked out just right. We continued working through 1993 to prepare for 1994 MIPCOM. We had a buyer list from our last MIPCOM. Howard sent letters with our information to many different countries. In 1994 the people who received our letter made appointments with our company. The second year was much better; we picked up more clients.

*****

Eurosport Television Network called Howard and asked for our demo tape. This established our tapes in the European market. We made only a little money, but we established ourselves. We were looking for the market in Europe. Once our tapes showed on Eurosport, they saw the intensity of our shows, very close contact. People saw WWF/WWE and WCW on different channels. They compared the two companies with ours, the Japanese style wrestling, naturally because the tapes are from Japan. The Japanese style wrestling is like American wrestling 15 to 20 years ago when I was wrestling. The people saw the difference between our show and their shows.

Our ratings passed the WWF/WWE and WCW shows. Eurosport was very happy. They carried our show more than 16 weeks. They were going to continue the show, but there was an internal struggle. They said wrestling was not a real sport. Our show was discontinued. Our ratings were better than other shows they were carrying. Unfortunately, we could not continue to produce without Eurosport. Even if we had other customers, we did not have enough money for production.

We had a customer in Singapore, ESPN in Asia. They carried our show in the Indian continent reaching about four different countries. They carried us for about one year. Then, they merged with another channel that carried the WWF/WWE shows. They had to discontinue our show. Unfortunately, many things happened to block our success.

*****

Europe is a great market. It is wide open. No one is promoting locally. We are looking for some opportunity. If we had the funding, I would be there tomorrow to promote. In the early 1960's to 1972, the European market was great. I had many friends that before coming to the United States wrestled in Europe. I met Ciclon Negro in Houston in 1961. He broke my left ankle. Before coming to the

United States, he spent four years in France, making good money. He was a young man from Venezuela. He went to France four years, then back to Venezuela, then to the United States. Also, Don Curtis, who is a good friend of mine, told me he used to sell out Paris every month in 1954. In England, Gordon Nelson, whom I met in 1962 in Oklahoma, worked as a referee and carried the ring until 1987. He brought a Mercedes Benz from England. Everyone told me the market in Europe is great. The opportunity is there.

*****

We went to MIPCOM Exhibition three years in a row, 1993, 1994, and 1995. The exhibition was costing so much money, $16,000 to rent the booth, $6,000 for decorating the booth. Then the hotel, the transportation. All together it cost almost $30,000. The fourth year we went to another exhibition, SPORTEL, just for sports held in Monte Carlo. That exhibition fee was only $6,000.

In 1996, we went to SPORTEL instead of MIPCOM. SPORTEL ran after MIPCOM; most people went to both. SPORTEL was small compared to MIPCOM, because it was only sports. The exhibition was four days long.

We stayed at a nice hotel called Hotel Metropol. One day I was coming down the elevator to the lobby. An Asian man came onto the elevator. We looked at each other. I knew right away that he was Japanese. We did not speak, just showed our respect.

Later on during the sport exhibition, he showed up at my booth with another Japanese man. He asked, "Are you Hiro Matsuda? When I saw you in the hotel, you looked like Mr. Matsuda, but I did not want to make a mistake. That is why I did not say hello to you." He introduced himself as Mr. Seiki. He has an office in Tokyo. He has been coming to SPORTEL for several years. He invited Howard and me to dinner after the show that day. He had a restaurant he liked to go to when he was at SPORTEL. We accepted the invitation.

Monte Carlo is built by the ocean on a hill. The restaurant was located by the beach. We had to go down the street from our hotel on the hill. We got to the restaurant about nine-thirty at night. We sat down and ordered wine. There were not many people yet. At ten-thirty, more people started coming into the restaurant.

Mr. Seiki knew me. He is one year younger than I. He used to work for Tokyo Sports with some old friends of mine. He knew everybody. We became well acquainted, because we had so much in common. We were talking about old times. After a few drinks, we started singing war songs from our childhood. Songs from World War II.

The most popular song of our age was called "Tokkotai" about the kamikaze, the suicide pilots. We started singing. There were not too many people in the place. We really enjoyed it.

After dinner we ate a nice dessert with zambukas. It is a sweet Italain after dinner drink. Then, on the way to the hotel, we found a Mexican restaurant and bar. We stopped by and ordered tequila. The people spoke Spanish. We had a few tequila together. Then, we were holding each other, walking shoulder to shoulder, singing the war song all the way back to the hotel. That is a wonderful memory. I promised to go back the next year, but unfortunately we could not afford to go. In the future, if we have a financial investor, we will be in Europe. Also, we will be participating in all those kinds of exhibitions. That is my dream.

*****

Last year, 1998, a potential investor expressed interest in our show. We sent the contract, but it was never signed. There were several partners running many different businesses with the investment money. The deal did not go through because of some mistake, some miscommunication. It was extended to this year. We are told the deal is not dead; it will still go through. So far we have not seen any funding in our account. Last conversation Howard had with the investor, we were assured the deal is still on. But, when?

If, I do not want to use if, I will say when. When the deal comes through, we will have the office in London. Our plan is to run all the European big cities. That is our dream. I wish before I die, I'd like to have one more dream happen, my last dream. This deal started in 1998, to the present in 1999. The investor could say the deal is off, but he insists it is still on. I have to believe the man. If I do not believe him, there is nothing I can believe in anymore.

I guess timing is everything. When I got sick, there is some reason. There was some reason the deal was postponed. Life has a very funny way of working. Before they discovered my cancer, I was edgy because I was very angry. The deal was promised, but it had not gone through yet. There were many nights I could not sleep because of the anxiety. After I discovered my cancer, nothing is important anymore. Life is more precious than any one thing in life. My attitude has changed completely about life. I take each day. If the deal comes through, fine. I have more thinking on business. If the deal comes through, the business will be very successful, because I am not greedy like I was before, and now I can cooperate more with anybody. In order to make the business successful, I have the right mind now.

Regarding the investor, he could say anytime that the deal is over, because he is handling the finances. However, he keeps saying that the deal is on. I have to believe him. He has nothing to gain by telling me and telling Howard the deal is still on. Therefore, I have to believe something.

If the funding comes through, I have a great plan. This is my last wrestling experience, my grand finale of the wrestling business. I started when I was nineteen years old to become the biggest professional wrestler in the world. I made a success, my dream. Also, I became a promoter. I learned business method through different businesses I participated in. Therefore, if I have this opportunity come, I know I will make a great success. People will see Hiro Matsuda from all over the world, running wrestling from London. If the funding does not come through, then I did not lose anything. This is an extra part of my wrestling career; therefore, I do not regret anything. However, if the money comes through the saga of Hiro Matsuda will flourish, the last chapter of Hiro Matsuda.

I can see having a couple custom made buses carrying young wrestlers from all over the world, going to different cities. Tonight, Paris. Tomorrow, Amsterdam. Just I can visualize. It brings me back to when I was young. Boys of 19, 20, 25 years getting on the bus, pursuing the same dream I had. I would like to give the opportunity to those young people like I had, like people gave me opportunity.

When I stare at the map of Europe, there are so many different countries, but the distance between them is not far, like running from Tampa to Jacksonville to Miami. If you go 500 miles, you would be in a different country, even just 200 miles just crossing the border in

Europe, speak a different language. But to me, I wrestled all over the United States. The United States is bigger than Europe.

Life in Europe would be totally different than in the United States. Just crossing the border, the customs are different, people are different, the language is different, the food is different. I like the very cosmopolitan and continental way of living. Therefore, if I have the opportunity, I will really enjoy living in the European style.

*****

Life works in a funny way. Like I said earlier, if the money came through yesterday or the day before yesterday, my mindset was different. There is some reason. Always, there is some reason in life. Maybe I am superstitious, but life always has some reason to fitting the pieces into the puzzle. You never know. I am living one day at a time. I get up in the morning; I appreciate God giving me an extra day, so I am not wasting any minute, any hour. When I get up, I plan what I am going to do today. So far, I am enjoying every minute.

*****

November 27, 1999 Hiro Matsuda took his last breath with his wife and daughters by his side. His grand finale dream did not come to fruition, but he died with peace in his heart. His friends called him a Samurai Spirit. He set his mind and heart on something, and he never wavered. He was honorable, determined, and loyal. Even with his cancer treatment, he set his path. He fought whole heartedly at first. He received chemotherapy. He ate a macrobiotic diet. He tried alternative therapies. He was determined to win. However, no treatment touched the cancer. There was no change. At this time he asked, "Why keep fighting if there is no change? I want to eat what I want and enjoy my days." He did not want to try a stronger chemotherapy treatment with harsher side effects. He felt it would not give him more time. He chose quality of life. He wanted to enjoy all the foods he loved and enjoy each day as much as possible with his family. When his day to die came, so be it. He died as he had lived.

*****

In 2018 Hiro Matsuda was inducted into the Professional Wrestling Hall of Fame in Wichita Falls, Texas and the WWE Legacy Hall of Fame. His memoir completes the saga of Hiro Matsuda. He will be remembered forever by those who love him.

ABOUT THE AUTHOR

Stephanie Kojima was determined to fulfill her father's wish to publish his memoir. She lives in Tampa, Florida.

Made in the USA
Las Vegas, NV
05 April 2021